Henry Theophilus Finck

Wagner Handbook for the Festival Concerts Given in 1884

Henry Theophilus Finck

Wagner Handbook for the Festival Concerts Given in 1884

ISBN/EAN: 9783337386634

Printed in Europe, USA, Canada, Australia, Japan

Cover: Foto ©Thomas Meinert / pixelio.de

More available books at **www.hansebooks.com**

WAGNER HANDBOOK

FOR THE

Festival Concerts

GIVEN IN 1884 UNDER THE DIRECTION OF

THEODORE THOMAS

ANALYTIC PROGRAMMES WITH ENGLISH TEXTS
BIOGRAPHIC AND CRITICAL ESSAYS

BY

HENRY T. FINCK

PROJECTOR AND MANAGER OF THE CONCERTS

CHARLES E. LOCKE

With Illustrations

CAMBRIDGE
JOHN WILSON AND SON
University Press
1884

Wagner Concerts.

—◆—

Musical Director.

MR. THEODORE THOMAS.

Sopranos.

FRAU AMALIA FRIEDRICH-MATERNA,
Court Singer of the Imperial Opera, Vienna,

MISS EMMA JUCH,

MISS HATTIE LOUISE SIMMS,	MISS ELLA EARLE,
MISS ZELIE DE LUSSAN,	MISS FANNIE HIRSCH,
MRS. MINNIE E. DENNISTON,	MRS. A. HARTDEGEN,

AND

MADAME CHRISTINE NILSSON.

Contralto.

MISS EMILY WINANT.

Tenors.

HERR HERMANN WINKELMANN,	MR. THEODORE TOEDT.
Court Singer of the Imperial Opera, Vienna.	MR. JACOB GRAFF.

Basses.

HERR EMIL SCARIA,	MR. FRANZ REMMERTZ.
Court Singer of the Imperial Opera, Vienna.	MR. MAX TREUMANN.

DR. CARL E. MARTIN.

C. M. WISKE — Chorus Master.

New York Chorus Society. — Brooklyn Philharmonic Chorus.

Male Chorus of the New York Liederkranz.

Grand Orchestra of 150 Musicians.

WAGNER IN THE CONCERT HALL.

S it advisable to play selections from Wagner's music-dramas in the Concert Hall? Theoretically, Wagner was opposed to this proceeding; and it is easy to see why. The old-fashioned opera is merely a series of arias, duos, quartets, recitatives, and choruses, which have no connection whatever with each other, and any one of which can therefore be produced as a complete concert-piece. But Wagner abandoned these disjointed forms, with rare exceptions. His operas are built up on a higher and more organic principle, each part being connected with every other by means of the continuous melody and the ever-recurring and newly combined leading motives. These motives first appear as mere melodic germs or buds; then they gradually grow and unfold themselves, until, when the climax is reached, we have the full-blown flower. To cut out a part of this organism is like cutting out a single figure from an exciting dramatic scene by a great artist. We see and admire the expression of this figure, but we fail to see the cause of it, and in so far must remain unsatisfied.

There is, however, another side to this question, which Wagner apparently recognized in practice. Between 1860, when he gave three concerts in Paris which cost him ten thousand francs, and the great London concerts in 1877, he took part, directly or indirectly, in various series of concerts at which selections from all his operas were produced. The object was partly to secure funds for his Bayreuth project, and partly to create an interest in his operas and a demand for their performance. He arranged various selections from his dramas for concert purposes; and Wagner concerts have accordingly become a regular feature of musical life in all the German capitals, as well as in Paris and in London, where the largest halls often do not suffice to hold all who apply for tickets when Hans Richter conducts.

In "Parsifal" the music, poetry, action, and scenery are so inseparably united that very little has been found available for concert purposes, although in its proper place

RICHARD WAGNER.

the music is sublime. But all the preceding dramas contain pieces — such as the forest scene from "Siegfried," the trio of the Rhine daughters in "Götterdämmerung," the love duo in "Tristan and Isolde," the Magic Fire scene in the "Walküre," the *Siegfried* funeral music — that are admirably suited for concert performance ; not to speak of the overtures to the "Flying Dutchman," "Tannhäuser," "Meistersinger," "Tristan," which are complete symphonic poems or miniature dramas in themselves, like Beethoven's great "Leonora" overture. One advantage of giving Wagner in the concert-hall lies in this : that his best thoughts only are presented, while all those parts are omitted which a mixed audience finds monotonous, — although a connoisseur finds even here something to interest him, in details of harmonization and instrumentation.

In listening to some of the most inspired passages, — such as occur in the second act of "Tristan," — the hearer is so overwhelmed by the richness and grandeur of the music that he feels as if it were enough in itself, and everything else — action and scenery — an intrusion. This feeling passes away when the whole work becomes more familiar ; but it shows what is of importance to remember, — that Wagner's music, even if it loses some of its effect in the concert-hall, is yet, when at its best, equal to the finest works written by other masters especially for the concert-hall.

EARLY WORKS FOR CONCERT PERFORMANCE.

NOTHING affords a more striking proof of the grandeur of Wagner's genius than the observation, which every one must make in listening to his operas, that the beauty and power of his music invariably increase with the impressiveness of the poetry and the dramatic situation. Minor composers are satisfactory in ordinary situations, but fail when they come to a scene of thrilling interest. Wagner is at his best where most is expected. The boiling-point of his emotional thermometer is many degrees higher than that of any other dramatic composer. "Tristan and Isolde" reveals deeper depths of tragic passion, of intense and sustained emotion, than the works of any dramatist except Shakespeare. When the subject becomes uninteresting, Wagner's musical art also sinks, but never to the level of the commonplace. Even the weakest of all his works, the "Festival March," which he wrote to order for the Centennial at Philadelphia, is anything but commonplace. It is a poor composition, because, never having been in America, he had no definite images to stimulate his imagination. Ordinarily, poetry, scenery, and music appear to have been present in his mind at the same time. When he wrote for the concert-stage he hardly ever attained the grandeur that pervades his music-dramas. On these dramas — eleven in number, counting from "Rienzi" to

" Parsifal " — rest his claims to immortality. The number of his works not written for the theatre is larger than is generally known. Most of them belong to his earliest period. A dozen or more have remained in manuscript, including nine overtures, selections from early operas preceding " Rienzi," a sonata, a quartet, a sextet, and a New Year's cantata. Among those that have been printed are a polonaise, two sonatas, and two album-pieces for the piano, several songs, " Siegfried Idyl," an early symphony, " Liebesmhal der Apostel," several orchestral marches, and a funeral march on motives from Weber's " Euryanthe."

A MASTER OF ORCHESTRAL EFFECTS.

PERFECT human voice is the noblest of all instruments. But perfect voices are exceedingly rare, while perfect violins and pianos are abundant. This may partly explain why the two composers who have had the most refined ears for exquisite sound effects, Chopin and Wagner, were at their best when writing instrumental music. The timbre of the human voice, like the blueness of the sky, is capable of considerable variety of shading, but it always retains its quality ; while the hues and tints of the orchestra have all the fascinating variety and charm of gorgeous sunsets, no two of which are alike. Every instrument, it may be said, has its special emotional character. The flute is serene, pastoral ; the violin gay, like major, the cello sad, like minor ; the bassoon, lugubrious in slow movement, humorous in rapid passages ; the trumpet, martial ; the trombones, stately, grand, majestic ; the harp, ethereal, celestial. No composer ever understood these peculiarities so thoroughly as Wagner. When Liszt wrote his admirable analysis of "Lohengrin," after its first performance, in 1850, under his direction, he called attention to the fact that Elsa is almost always accompanied by wind instruments, the King by the trombones and trumpets, while the Grail motive (as subsequently in " Parsifal ") is assigned to the violins.

Technically, Berlioz was almost as great a master of instrumentation as Wagner ; but his delicious effects often seem to exist for their own sake, without having any underlying idea, while Wagner's are always the outgrowth of the situation. Many have endeavored to copy Wagner's colors, but few have succeeded. It can be shown on acoustic principles why it is that a certain passage sounds well if played by a certain combination of instruments, and less effective if played by others. To know which ones to choose requires a special instinct, which cannot be acquired, but is innate, like the poet's genius.

Wagner's Dramatic Instinct.

To Wagner's mind a musical idea presented itself at once in its proper color ; while most musicians make a mere pen-and-ink sketch at first, and leave the choice of colors to subsequent deliberation.

Wagner was not satisfied with the symphonic orchestra of his day, but added to it some obsolete but useful instruments, and introduced in others the latest scientific improvements. Like some of the operatic reformers that preceded him, — Monteverde, Gluck, Mozart, — he gave the orchestra greater prominence than it had had before, and, like them, was consequently accused of being " too noisy." It cannot be denied that he does make more use of the brass than any other composer ; but it is generally used *pianissimo*, for the sake of obtaining new effects of color, and not to create a noise. His operatic predecessors chiefly used the brass for the sake of noise ; and it was consequently some time before the musicians understood him, and learned to play softly. At present, complaints are seldom heard that Wagner is too noisy, and many are surprised, especially on hearing " Tristan " and " Parsifal," at the infrequency of loud passages.

One of Wagner's epoch-making innovations was the practice of dividing instruments into several family groups, — strings, wood-wind, brass, instruments of percussion, — and completing the groups with new instruments whenever necessary. With each class and sub-class of instruments he was thus enabled to attain homogeneous effects, like those of a quartet of human voices, a quartet of cellos, violins, etc. ; and to the variety of novel combinations thus secured are due the kaleidoscopic changes of his orchestration. One instance of a new effect, with which every one is familiar, occurs in the " Lohengrin " prelude, where the flutes and divided solo violins, in their highest position, give an ethereal tint to the Grail motive which makes it appear like a true halo of sound.

WAGNER'S DRAMATIC INSTINCT.

NO writer for the stage has ever had a keener sense for legitimate theatric effect than Wagner. The dramatic instinct came to him by inheritance. His father was greatly devoted to the stage, and occasionally appeared as an amateur actor. He died when Richard was only half a year old. Ludwig Geyer, who became his step-father two years later, was an actor as well as a painter. Wagner's oldest brother, Albert, was well known as an actor and stage manager in Berlin ; his daughter, Johanna Jachmann Wagner, became a famous vocalist and actress. Early in life Richard manifested great interest in the stage. The " Freischütz " was his favorite opera, and Weber his idol, — which he remained to the end of his life, although Bach, Beethoven, Gluck, Mozart, and Palestrina had an equal share of his admiration. In one of his autobiographic sketches Wagner says that in his youth he had an inclination to act, and gratified it in his own room. "Coupled with this, however, was a peculiar disinclina-

17

tion to go on the stage; early impressions of classic antiquity and its seriousness, which I received at school, may have inspired in me a certain contempt, — yes, even an abhorrence, — of the painted comedians and their doings." Probably an instinctive perception of the shortcomings of the operatic singers of that period may have had something to do with this abhorrence, which subsequently led him to devote so much time to the task of converting puppet tenors and prima donnas into real actors and actresses.

CRITICISM AND PREJUDICE.

IKE all great reformers, Wagner occasionally used extravagant language in expressing his opinions; and this, combined with the malicious misrepresentations of his enemies, helped to foster a general belief that he insolently despised all the great masters who preceded him, as well as contemporary musicians. His opinion of the latter, indeed, was not very high, owing to the fact that they must have seemed to him to be either imitators and plagiarists of his own style and ideas, or else given to lyric and symphonic tendencies, with which he had no more sympathy than Mendelssohn had with his dramatic instinct, or Handel with Bach's harmonic depth and originality. But to assert that Wagner disparaged the great masters of the past, is simply to display a complete ignorance of his opinions. "I believe in God, Mozart, and Beethoven," was an early confession of his faith; and his admiration for Beethoven, Weber, Liszt, Palestrina, Bach, and a few other composers was unbounded to his last days. He did indeed have the boldness and sense of justice to put his finger on the weak spots of his idols no less than of others; and these isolated opinions have often been dishonestly quoted without their context.

His opponents found it very easy to misrepresent his views, because they are embodied in no less than ten volumes, containing 3,988 pages, which few have had the courage to examine carefully. They contain, besides his dramatic texts, a few occasional poems and several semi-autobiographic musical novelettes, a large number of critical papers, and several long treatises, devoted, with a few insignificant exceptions, to musical and dramatic subjects. Some of these treatises and essays are written in such a turgid and complicated style that his greatest admirers are frightened away from them, and Wagner himself confessed subsequently that he could not re-read them. Their fault is one common to German writers, — that of putting thoughts on paper before they have assumed a clear, crystalline form. In the present case this fault is of interest, because it shows that Wagner did not premeditate his operatic reforms, but gradually deduced them from the outcome of his spontaneous, creative genius in his operas.

In the majority of these essays, however, the reader finds a directness of statement, a nervous vigor of style, and an acute perception, which leave no doubt that the author

18

was the most incisive musical critic the world has ever seen. The historic sketch of the opera which is contained in the third volume of his collected works is a master-piece of critical literature, and contains opinions which all the world is gradually but surely indorsing. In conjunction with others of the essays, it constitutes such a treasure of information and suggestion for the student of æsthetics and music that these ten volumes may be safely placed on the same shelf with Lessing's "Dramaturgie."

A FINE PICTORIAL SENSE.

HERE can be no doubt that if Wagner had not chosen to be a composer and dramatist, he might have become one of the greatest of modern painters. A German critic, in discussing the tetralogy, says that "it is especially the pictorial sense of Wagner that is at work incessantly in the Nibelungen ; it appears to have furnished the first impulse for many of the scenes. In looking at the photographs of Joseph Hoffmann's poetically conceived decorations, the thought involuntarily occurs, that such pictures may have arisen first in Wagner's imagination and brought forth the corresponding music." The first scene in "Rheingold," where we see the three Rhine daughters swimming about under the water, a section of which occupies the whole stage to the top, and appears to flow on steadily; the wild maidens, in the "Walküre," riding among the clouds and alighting on precipitous rocks, filling the air with their weird song ; the forest scene in "Siegfried," where the hero lies under a tree with spreading branches, and listens to the song of the birds and the rustling of the leaves, so beautifully imitated by the orchestra ; the final scene of the "Götterdämmerung," where the river begins to rise and inundate the ruins of the hall, bearing on its swelling waves the Rhine daughters once more, and accompanied by the surging sounds of the symphonic flood ; the magnificent ecclesiastic scenes in "Parsifal," which are like pictures of the old Italian masters brought to life, — these and a score of other scenes bear witness to Wagner's pictorial genius; for all these scenes are described in detail in his text-books, leaving the scene-painter no further task than the execution of his minute directions. In this *penchant* for artistic conceptions Wagner resembles Goethe. It is interesting to note, too, that his stepfather was a painter, and wanted Richard to become an artist. But the process of learning the technique did not suit his fancy, and he soon abandoned the brush in favor of the poet-musician's pencil.

19

A MANY-SIDED SPECIALIST.

ODERN artistic life, like modern industry, tends toward division of labor and specialization. Chopin, Franz, and Wagner are conspicuous instances of this tendency. Chopin is, *par excellence*, the poet of the pianoforte ; for other instruments he wrote but little. Franz has created a few works of large dimensions, but his claim to immortality rests on his 250 songs, in which are united some of the best qualities of Bach, Schumann, and Schubert. Wagner was born for the stage, and devoted his whole life to it. Even when engaged in literary work, his object always was to promote the interests of the music-drama. In one sense, however, Wagner was the direct opposite of a specialist. He was not a musician alone, like Haydn, Mozart, and Beethoven, but a poet, dramatist, and stage-manager as well. As an ideal dramatist he required all these qualities ; for the true specialist is not he who takes up only one branch of his subject, but he who devotes himself to every cognate subject that may be of use in his general scheme. Wagner must not be judged, therefore, by his music alone. The perfume of a rose is sweet in itself, but sweeter still when we can see the beautiful flower that exhales it.

LEADING MOTIVES.

T is well known that Wagner was not the first who made use of leading motives or representative themes. Isolated cases occur in Berlioz and Meyerbeer, and a very beautiful example is introduced in Weber's " Euryanthe,"— an opera which is in many respects the direct precursor of " Lohengrin," and of which Wagner wrote a few years before his death that " every single number is worth more than all the *opera seria* of Italy, France, and Judæa." It remained for Wagner's dramatic instinct to perceive the utility of this new device, and develop it into a new variety of musical form, the importance of which cannot be over-estimated.

Darwinism presents an analogous case. Darwin was by no means the first to announce that the higher forms of life are developed from the lower. A few years ago, in fact, a German professor published a treatise on the ancient Greek predecessors of Darwin. But Darwin was the first who had the acuteness to perceive that this theory alone accorded with all the known biological facts, as well as the tremendous array of new ones which he collected to prove it, while endeavoring at the same time

Leading Motives.

to account for it on the hypothesis of natural selection. If the principle of development and the use of leading motives had never suggested themselves to thinkers and artists before Darwin and Wagner, they would have lost one of the greatest arguments · in their favor. And it is well to remember that some of the greatest achievements of men of genius often consist in developing germs of ideas in the works of their predecessors, while they in turn leave incidental suggestions for future men of genius to elaborate into a system.

For every dramatic personage or important factor in the plot Wagner invented a musical passage or motive, which recurs again and again in the course of the drama, whenever a significant act occurs or is referred to in the poem. These motives are always characterized by a realism and pictorial suggestiveness which no other composer has equalled. Compare, for instance, the weird, unearthly leading motive of the *Dutchman* with the seductive strains of the sirens in "Tannhäuser;" the dreamy, tender music of *Elsa* with the majestic strains of the *King;* or the heavy, clumsy motive of the giants in "Rheingold" with the voices of the forest in "Siegfried;" and imagine all these as being interchanged: the result would be ludicrous.

These leading motives are by no means always affixed to a character on the stage, like a musical label, but only appear when the situation calls for them. Nor are they stereotyped musical phrases. They undergo constant changes in rhythm, harmony, time, and instrumentation, and often two or more of them are combined in a very effective manner and with rare polyphonic skill. By changing from a sombre to a bright instrumental color, from slow to quick time, from major to minor, Wagner alters the emotional character of the same motive, to suit the momentary mood of the personage represented by it. More than this: in a moment of happiness a motive typical of an evil influence is introduced with thrilling effect, as a presentiment of an impending tragedy; or again, a musical phrase connected with a former experience is subsequently introduced, and brings with it all its associations and sentiments.

Wagner's use of leading motives thus adds to music a new psychologic power of inestimable value; and, what is of equal importance, these motives form a bond of union between the different parts of the drama, which the old-fashioned opera entirely lacks, since there we have a series of unconnected arias, duos, and choruses, which are sung once and never recur. This is very much as if a dramatist made each of his characters say what he has to say, and then dropped him from the play; or as if he combined a dozen plays, each lasting fifteen minutes, and each having its own characters and its own plot. Although each of these plays might be a gem, no one would call the whole a work of art; and it is for a similar reason that Wagner abandoned the old operatic form and created a new one.

Music is the language of emotion. It expresses many of the æsthetic emotions with a force not equalled by any other art. But it cannot express a special case of emotion, as the love of Romeo for Juliet. It must therefore be combined with explanatory poetry and a pictorial background, as in the music-drama, in order to attain its most powerful effects. Wagner, however, has succeeded in giving music a wonderful secondary definiteness by means of the leading motives. After hearing his dramas once or twice, we remember with what person or incident each motive is associated, and it is therefore possible to follow the whole plot by listening to the music alone.

TRAGEDY AND DISCORD.

RAGEDY had a greater fascination for Wagner than comedy. "Die Meistersinger" and "Siegfried" are the only ones of his dramas in which the comic element becomes conspicuous, although even here it is accompanied by a strong under-current of tragedy. In the Italian operas of Rossini, Bellini, Donizetti, and in some of the German operas based on these models, it makes very little difference whether the story is cheerful or sad. In either case the composer's only aim is to furnish a series of sweet, dainty, pretty little tunes, intermingled with trills, scales, arpeggios and staccati, for the purpose of showing the audience how admirably the prima donna has trained the muscles of her vocal chords. Not so in the modern music-drama. Wagner does not write a waltz when some one is dying on the stage. His music, from beginning to end, follows not only the general emotional character of the situation, but clings closely to every line and every word, as is the case in those modern songs of Schumann, Liszt, Franz, in which every verse has its own music, instead of being a mere echo of that of the preceding verse. No one can have an adequate idea of the intimate union that is possible between music and poetry until he has followed the music of "Tristan and Isolde" with the text-book on his knees, or has heard it interpreted by such singers as Materna, Winkelmann, and Scaria, who pronounce their consonants distinctly, without sacrificing the beauty of their vowel tones.

In carrying out the principle of making the music follow the sense of the poetry, the dramatic subject naturally conditions the character of the music. Wagner's subjects are sad and tragic, therefore his music is sad and tragic. It is full of discords, and not always "beautiful." This offends the taste of those who are brought up under the Italian opera *régime*. They insist on having sweet and beautiful music under all circumstances. Their system of musical æsthetics might be called the sugar-candy theory. If they should attempt to apply it to the literary drama, they would see how ridiculous it is. King Lear is not beautiful, neither is Othello. The emotions inspired by them are those of tragic passion, grandeur, power, pity, pathos, sadness; but not the tender emotions which accompany the Beautiful. In the songs assigned to *Eva, Senta, Elsa,* Wagner has shown that no one can write more beautiful music than he; but when he comes to discordant passages he uses discords, because discords and modulations alone can express tragic passions. Just as a dramatist in the midst of a thrilling situation does not break the spell by letting some one prematurely tell how it is all going to end, so Wagner avoids cadences and premature concords, and passes on from one discord to another, thus keeping the feelings of the hearer at a high state of tension until the end is reached.

From the severe and apparently sincere condemnation of modern dissonances pronounced by conservative critics, one may infer that they actually give them physical pain. This is to be regretted; but if they will consult a history of music, they will find that conservatives were always thus affected whenever an epoch-making composer enlarged the possibilities of harmonic combinations. The younger generation of musicians love Wagner's discords and modulations, as they do those of Chopin, because they afford a glimpse into hitherto unsuspected relationships between remote keys; for discord is but "harmony ill understood." They love them also because to them they owe the æsthetic pleasure of sadness, which is so much more intense than the pleasure of joy.

WAGNER'S POETRY.

EINRICH HEINE is reported to have once said in conversation: "Do you know what I find suspicious in Wagner? The fact that he is recommended by Meyerbeer." Yet Meyerbeer, with all his faults and his inordinate anxiety to please the public, had a genuine dramatic sense, and always kept his eyes open for something that promised theatric success. When he became acquainted with the poem "Rienzi," he pronounced it the best opera libretto known to him, and requested Scribe to furnish him one of a similar structure. But "Rienzi" is by far the poorest of Wagner's dramatic texts. Its successor, "The Flying Dutchman," marks such a great advance, that Liszt was induced to write that "the whole arrangement of the text-book betrays a genuine artist, a poet by the grace of God, a hand of which every line, every stroke of the pen, rises far above the opera-texts hitherto known." In Paris, where Wagner vainly endeavored to secure an order to produce the "Dutchman," he nevertheless succeeded in disposing of the libretto for five hundred francs. In "Tannhäuser" and "Lohengrin" dramatic power and poetic beauty become still more conspicuous, so that more than one of the author's musical enemies looked with longing eyes on his literary productions. Wagner's own brother Albert considered him a much greater poet than composer, and Schopenhauer once exclaimed: "This fellow is a poet, not a musician," — as might have been expected of one who considered Rossini the greatest of all composers.

In some of his later dramas, notably "Tristan" and "Götterdämmerung," Wagner introduced a considerable amount of Schopenhauer's metaphysical speculation. This is out of place in a stage-play, and constitutes a weakness of the later as compared with the earlier dramas. It makes some passages obscure to the general reader or spectator, although those who are familiar with Schopenhauer experience no difficulty. Now that Wagner is dead, the suggestion that his poems should be studied, like those of other great poets, will perhaps be no longer considered so very insolent and unreasonable. His love for archaic expressions in these later dramas has been greatly exaggerated. It has been proved by actual count that Goethe used many more such expressions than he; whereas it is evident that a musical poet has much more justification for such a thing than a literary poet. In Wagner's art-work music has to make many concessions to poetry, and it is but fair that poetry, in turn, should make some concessions. Much sarcasm has been expended on the first lines of "Rheingold," where the Rhine daughters swim, and sing: —

"Weia! Waga! Woge, du Welle, walle zur Wiege, Wagalaweia, Wallala, weiala, weia!"

In print this does look ludicrous; but in its proper place, accompanied by the graceful, waving song of the maidens, it has an exquisitely realistic effect. It is a kind of artistic onomatopœia, like other passages in these dramas. The last song of *Isolde* is one of the most marvellous poems ever written. It is the only known instance where a writer has succeeded in conveying in words all the intense pathos and sadness of the music itself.

In much of his poetry Wagner abandoned rhyme in favor of alliteration. Rhyme is a consonance of sounds at the end of lines, which appears primitive and almost childish, when compared with the endless variety of musical sounds and combinations in an opera. Its absence is therefore not missed; whereas, if present, it frequently leads to incorrect accentuation. Alliteration, on the contrary, is of immense advantage in dramatic poetry. How well the repetition of the *w* in the "Weia! Waga!" expresses the swimming motion of the Rhine daughters. A little later in the drama, *Alberich* attempts to capture one of them, but slides on the slippery slime, as his words indicate: —

"Garstig glatter glitschriger Glimmer! Wie gleit' ich aus!"

One does not need to understand German to feel the onomatopoetic force of these words. So in many other passages that might be quoted. Every emotion has an affinity for certain consonants, and it is by studying these affinities that Wagner, for the first time, taught vocal music to express the whole scale of emotions, — not only the tender feelings. Anger, hatred, jealousy, are in the tones of *Alberich's* and *Mime's* voices in "Siegfried," when they contend for the treasure. This surely is something new under the sun; it enlarges the sphere of music. And it is worthy of note that Wagner somewhere quotes without disapproval the remark, that his music-dramas are less the outgrowth of the opera than of the melodrama, in which spoken words are accompanied by the orchestra, while he makes melodious declamation take the place of the spoken words.

A NEW VOCAL STYLE.

T is worthy of special notice that Mozart and Weber, in the most dramatic situations of their operas, make use of a vocal style which distinctly foreshadows Wagner's melodious declamation. In the heat of inspiration they felt for the moment what Wagner's acute theatric sense at once told him was the only true method of dramatic singing. The gradual development of this new style can be easily followed in his operas. Traces of it are seen in " Rienzi," and with each succeeding opera it gains in ease and power, until, in " Parsifal," the part of *Gurnemanz* may be said to represent the perfection of vocal art, in which distinctness of speech and melodious flow and beauty of tone are united in a manner never before dreamed of.

It would be absurd to maintain that this new style is destined to replace all other styles. Wagner, indeed, believed that both the literary drama and absolute music would disappear in the course of time as separate arts, and become merged in the music-drama, — the " art-work of the future." But other mortals, whose interests are not all centred on the stage, may be permitted to doubt this prophecy. Lyric song certainly will never be allowed to fall into neglect. The folk-songs of all nations, the songs of Schubert and other masters, and some of the airs of Italian opera composers will always be heard with pleasure in the parlor and the concert hall, although the latter will not be tolerated by future generations on the operatic stage. An advocate of Wagner, however, might claim that even the tendency of lyric music affords an argument in favor of his view. The vocal pieces of Schumann, Liszt, Franz, and other modern writers can hardly be called simple lyrics, but must be classed as " dramatic lyrics," because the cantabile style has been replaced by a declamatory style which closely resembles that of the music-drama, while the accompaniment also has assumed a character of greater complexity and dramatic significance.

Besides the lyric and dramatic styles, there is a third, the ornamental or florid, which was once almost absolute autocrat of the stage, but is now happily becoming obsolete, partly because taste has changed, and partly because there are no more vocalists who can do it justice. Mme. Patti is the only living vocalist who can sing without a flaw the difficult fioriture of Rossini, Donizetti, and Meyerbeer. In most cases these fioriture are not only ridiculously out of place where they are introduced, but they are decidedly vulgar. They only serve to show off the agility of a prima donna's vocal chords ; and the interest aroused in them is therefore athletic rather than æsthetic.

With a happy faculty for perverting facts, the lovers of ornamental, *rococo* singing insist that modern composers use the voice like an instrument. Quite the reverse. Those composers treated the voice like an instrument who constantly wrote for it passages which only one singer in a generation can execute, while for any second fiddle or flute the same passage would be mere child's play. In another respect, too, the Italian method of singing yields instrumental results. The alpha and omega of this method is a beautiful sensuous tone. In the endeavor to attain this, everything else is sacrificed, — striking melodic intervals, expressive consonants, and distinct pronunciation of words. But there is something higher in music than sensuous beauty of tone, and that is intellect, emotion, character. The greatest advantage which vocal music has over instrumental is that it can give definite utterance to poetic ideas and sentiments. This advantage the Italians sacrifice ; because, in the first place, their libretti are almost always silly, and, in the second, because they pay but little attention to anything but isolated vowels that show off the voice to the best advantage.

Can any one be so blind as not to see what an immense reform Wagner has brought about in this respect? His singers are engaged to appear in a drama ; and one of the first requisites, therefore, is that they should be able to act. They cannot act and display their vocal art at the same time ; therefore he does not ask them to display their vocal art. He simply asks them to phrase with intelligence, and interpret the poetry they are asked to sing in such a way that every word of it can be distinctly understood. As the melodic intervals are often difficult, they are obliged to familiarize themselves with the complete score, — that is, they have to be musicians, and not mere parrots who have never learned anything but solfeggios.

When singers first attempted this new style they generally failed. They sacrificed beauty of tone in the vain effort to pronounce distinctly ; and the consequence was a most dreary performance. But gradually the secrets of the new method were discovered, and the great singers who have thrice assembled at Bayreuth have triumphantly demonstrated the combined beauty and realism of Wagnerian song. This song is simply impassioned speech converted into an art. In listening to an emotional young lady, every one can hear how her voice rises and sinks. She speaks in melodic intervals. Salvini's inflections, it has been noticed, run over an interval of more than a fifth. From such facts as these we can infer the truth of Wagner's principles. Modern etiquette teaches us not to express our emotions by appearance and speech ; but it is the sphere of art to express what in life is thus forbidden. The music-drama is simply an amplification of natural phenomena, a reversion to primitive modes of utterance. Far from being artificial, it is less so than the spoken drama ; for, according to Darwin and Wagner, song, as an expression of emotion, comes before articulate speech.

26

EARLIEST OPERAS.

AGNER'S genius did not spring forth from his forehead Minerva-like, in full armor. He had to go through a long and disagreeable period of apprenticeship, and was twenty-nine years old when "Rienzi," the earliest of his operas which has kept the stage, was first produced (Dresden, 1842). "Rienzi" was preceded by at least four operatic projects, of which Wagner speaks briefly in his first autobiographic sketch. "The Wedding" was the name of the first; but as his sister did not approve of the text-book, he destroyed the whole thing. The next was "The Fairies," in which Beethoven and Weber were his prototypes. This was followed by "The Novice of Palermo," based on Shakespeare's "Measure for Measure." Then came a two-act comic opera, "The Happy Family of Bears," which he abandoned in disgust on discovering that he was again composing *à la* Adam. The fragments of these works that have been preserved are of no especial value, although some characteristic germs may be discovered in them.

An unprecedented extravagance and ambition appears to have been the most salient feature of Wagner's early compositions. One of his overtures, which he himself calls the culminating point of his absurdities, was produced at the Leipzig Theatre. The result of the performance was that the audience gradually passed from a state of amazement into an outbreak of general hilarity, which was stimulated by the recurrence, in every fourth bar throughout the overture, of a fortissimo drum-beat. To match this musical feat, he wrote, at about the same time, a terrific tragedy, in the course of which, he says, he killed off forty-two persons, so that toward the end the want of living characters compelled him to re-introduce most of them as ghosts. This was his "Storm and Stress period," as the Germans say. The best wine always has a period of violent fermentation.

"RIENZI."

F operatic rank were to be determined by the number of works each composer has written, Wagner, with his eleven operas and music-dramas, would come near the end of the list; while Donizetti, with his sixty-three operas, would probably rank first. In reality, there is more musical material in a single act of "Lohengrin" or "Tristan" than in a dozen or a score of the old-fashioned Italian operas, many of which were composed in a few weeks; while Wagner in most cases devoted several years to a new work, — the "Nibelungen" having, in fact, occupied him at intervals during a quarter of a century, being comparable in this respect to Goethe's "Faust."

"Rienzi" is the only one of his works which, if placed on its own merits, would probably soon disappear from the operatic repertory. As the predecessor of ten immortal dramas, it will always be revived at intervals, even if the interest in it should be historic rather than artistic. In regard to Wagner's attitude toward this work erroneous notions are current. He did not absolutely condemn it later in life, although, with a spirit of just self-criticism which is as rare as it is admirable, he pointed out his own shortcomings, just as he did those of other composers. In this opera, he says, he endeavored to surpass all the extravagant theatric effects and splendors of the French school of grand opera. In Bulwer's "Rienzi" he found a subject which readily adapted itself to the current style of operatic treatment. Effective finales, duos, trios, processions, presented themselves spontaneously, and in writing the poetry he bestowed on it no further thought and care than he considered necessary for the purposes of a good opera libretto.

Yet the subject did really inspire him, and in a foot-note he explains that he reprints the complete text in its original form, "as a means of correcting the judgment of those who know the opera only in the mutilated form in which it is now given in the theatres, and who are therefore astonished at the clumsy manner in which the grotesque effects are piled on one another." This quotation shows that he had a good word even for this wayward child of his; nor could he have overlooked some of those effective numbers which are symphonically united in the overture, and which contain distinct suggestions of his later harmonic and melodic peculiarities.

"THE FLYING DUTCHMAN."

IENZI was first produced on Oct. 20, 1842, at Dresden. Although the performance lasted six hours, the success of the new opera was great, and its most important consequence was that Wagner, who had hitherto been a poor struggling Bohemian, obtained the comfortable position of royal conductor at the Opera. "Rienzi" exactly suited the popular taste of the time, and if its author had continued to write in that style he would soon have rivalled Meyerbeer in popularity. But when "Rienzi" was produced he had already undergone a complete metamorphosis. Before he left Paris for Dresden he had completed "The Flying Dutchman" at Meudon, a small town near the French capital. This opera is shorter than his later works, and, contrary to his usual custom, he wrote it in quite a short time — about seven weeks. It contains the germs of most of his later reforms, — leading motives, a text of real poetic value in form and contents, a highly characteristic orchestral part, an unprecedented freedom in the use of discords and modulations, an avoidance of arias and orna-

THE ABDUCTION OF IRENE BY THE BARONS.

(Rienzi.)

mental vocalism. The acting assumed as much importance as the singing; and the scenery, instead of being dragged on the stage for mere effect, became the necessary background of the action.

No opera had ever been written in which there was such a unity amidst diversity of coloring, and such a close interweaving of parts. The audience, who had expected another spectacular opera like " Rienzi," were completely disappointed; and the same was the case in several other cities where " The Flying Dutchman " was produced. Among the few who appreciated it was the famous septuagenarian composer, Ludwig Spohr, who, as a musician, has little in common with Wagner, except a fondness for enharmonic changes of harmony. He heard the opera at Dresden, and caused it to be produced at Cassel. He wrote that he considered Wagner the most gifted dramatic composer of the period, whose aim was a noble one in a time when the common tendency was to produce mere startling effects and tickle the ears of the *vulgus*. He even went so far as to address a letter to Wagner, in which he expressed his joy at meeting with a young musician who showed in everything that art was a serious matter to him.

"TANNHÄUSER."

FTER a disappointment such as Wagner suffered in regard to " The Flying Dutchman," a less courageous composer would have altered his policy and endeavored to win back the confidence of the people. But Wagner knew that the mission of a genius is not to write down to the popular taste of his day, but to endeavor to elevate that taste to his own level. Had he essayed to adopt the style of Rossini, he would, like that composer, now be forgotten, or remembered by only one or two operas out of forty. As it was, he came within a year of living to hear the one-hundredth performance, amid enthusiastic acclamations, of "The Flying Dutchman," in the same city where, forty-two years before, it had proved a fiasco. He did live to see his operas head the list of annual performances in all the German capitals, and to witness the downfall of Italian opera, — which is now so complete that in Munich, Berlin, Hamburg, Leipzig, and other cities, where once it almost monopolized the stage, a whole month sometimes passes, in the midst of the season, during which not a single work by an Italian composer is given; while in Vienna it has repeatedly happened that the deficit left by a special series of Italian performances had to be covered with the receipts of a Wagner "cyclus." In America, too, in order to secure a full house, managers of Italian opera companies now have to produce on the same evening two *prime donne* of world-wide fame.

"Tannhäuser" marks an advance over "The Flying Dutchman," not as decided as in the preceding case, but still quite noticeable. There are in this opera at least two

" *Tannhäuser.* "

important passages — *Elisabeth's* prayer, and *Tannhäuser's* narrative on his return from Rome — which are characterized by all the wonderful declamatory naturalism and dramatic vigor of the vocal style in the later music-dramas. Like "The Flying Dutchman " and all subsequent works, with the exception of " Die Meistersinger," "Tannhäuser " is based on a mythic subject, — the story of the knight who was held captive in the mountain by the charms of Venus ; who subsequently seeks forgiveness of the Pope, which is refused ; and who is finally redeemed through the death of the pure maiden who loved him. This idea of the redeeming love of self-sacrificing woman is one which recurs in several of Wagner's dramas. It appears first in one of his earliest efforts, "The Fairies ;" it forms the keynote of "The Flying Dutchman ;" and is a conspicuous element of the later dramas. In " Lohengrin " it is introduced in a negative form, inasmuch as *Elsa* is punished because the curiosity and distrust inspired in her by *Ortrud* do not permit her to surrender herself unconditionally to the knight who came to save her. The self-surrendering love of woman typifies the union of music with poetry. One of Wagner's favorite maxims was that " Music is a woman." " A woman," he adds, " who does not love with the pride of absolute devotion, in reality does not love at all. But a woman who does not love at all is the most unworthy and repulsive object in the world." Wagner was fond of thus giving his dramatic plots a symbolic as well as an autobiographic interpretation.

The first performance of "Tannhäuser " was given at Dresden on Oct. 10, 1845, under the composer's own direction. The result was another great disappointment. At the second performance the house was only half full, and although subsequently matters improved so far that nine performances could be given up to the end of the year, yet it was not until after the appearance of Liszt's remarkable essay on " Tannhäuser," in 1859, that the opera began to make its way gradually throughout Germany. At Berlin it was first refused as being " too epic," just as the "Dutchman " had been previously refused at Munich as not being suited for the German stage. The general critical verdict was that " Tannhäuser " was monotonous, chaotic, the ephemeral production of an eccentric man. Liszt, however, came forward, boldly explained the peculiarities of Wagner's style, and proclaimed opinions which are now accepted throughout the civilized world. " As the text of ' Tannhäuser' is written with deep poetic feeling, and constitutes in itself an affecting drama, full of the most subtle shades of sentiment and passion ; as its plot is original and boldly conceived, the verses beautiful, often very beautiful, full of sudden flashes of sublime and powerful emotion, — so the music likewise is new, and demands special consideration." And again : " However great as a poet he may be, it is nevertheless only in the music that he finds the complete expression of his feelings, — so complete, in fact, that he alone is able to tell us whether he adapts his words to his melodies, or seeks melodies for his words."

ORTRUD ON HER KNEES BEFORE ELSA.

(LOHENGRIN.)

"LOHENGRIN."

F Liszt rendered valuable service in popularizing "Tannhäuser," still more was this the case with "Lohengrin,"
which was first performed under his direction at Weimar
on Aug. 28, 1850, the text having been completed in 1846
and the music in 1848. At this period of his life Wagner
had become so dissatisfied with the artistic life of the time,
that he concluded that a reform in theatric affairs could
only be attained through a general political convulsion ;
and he accordingly took part in the Revolution of May,
1849, and was in consequence obliged to leave the country
as a fugitive. On his way to Paris he stopped at Weimar,
where he heard a rehearsal of "Tannhäuser" under Liszt,
in whom he at once recognized his "second self," as he
expresses himself. "What I had felt in conceiving this
music he felt in executing it ; what I wished to express in
writing it, he announced in making it sound."

For two years and five months after its completion
"Lohengrin" remained unknown to the world ; when Wagner's eye fell on the "forgotten" manuscript. His previous scores had been so often returned to him, sometimes unopened, that he had almost lost hope that the world would ever understand
his new language. "Suddenly," he says, "I felt compassion for these tones on the
death-pale paper which were never to become a reality. Two words I wrote to Liszt ;
the answer to which was nothing less than the news that preparations for its performance were being made on the largest scale permitted by the limited resources of
Weimar." The first performance attracted the attention of all Germany, very much
as the Bayreuth festivals did in subsequent years ; but although some new friends
were won for the cause, the general public remained indifferent. Liszt accordingly
resorted to another weapon, — the pen of the critic and analyst ; and the result was
that wonderful essay on "Lohengrin," which accomplished for Wagner what Schumann's criticisms and prophecies did for Chopin and Brahms.

At the present day, when "Lohengrin" is known and admired throughout the
civilized world, it is easy to echo sentimental words of praise. But when Liszt first
spoke in favor of Wagner, the latter was regarded as an eccentric iconoclast, an enemy
of all that is true and beautiful in music ; and the verdict of criticism was quite as
hostile as a quarter of a century later in regard to the Nibelung tetralogy. It
required all the courage of his artistic conviction to enable Liszt boldly to place Wagner above Gluck, Weber, and all other opera composers, in regard to the essential
qualities required by a dramatic composer. He pointed out that the text is "a
dramatic work full of beauties of the highest order ; " that hereafter the habit of sup-
plying silly libretti to composers will be abolished ; that the difficulties of appreciating
these new operas lie not so much in their structure, as in the fact that singers and
audience alike are as yet unfamiliar with the new style ; that everything commonplace

is excluded ; that Wagner is not only conscientiously in love with art, but that "the noble and secret wound of fanaticism for art devours his heart ; " that in his eyes there are no singers, no *prima donna* or *basso cantante*, but only *rôles*, wherefore he finds it quite in order that the leading female singer should pause during a whole act, taking only a pantomimic part in the action ; that the orchestra mirrors and expresses the emotions, passions, and most subtle psychologic changes in his characters, — the utterance of hatred, the rage of revenge, the whispering of love, the ecstasy of worship.

These and many other things Liszt pointed out, thirty-four years ago, which are now universally conceded, but which at that time made the barbules of all the critical quills stand on end. History repeats itself. When the last part of the "Nibelungen" was first given in Vienna in 1879, the well-known critic, Dr. Hanslick, pathetically alluded to the "torture" of having to listen to all this stuff, and write about it too. Thirteen years before this another well-known critic, Otto Gumprecht, complained in a leading Berlin paper about the "cruel critical duty" which compelled him to listen to the "whining" and "chilling" music of "Lohengrin," and "to have his ears tortured during three hours by one of the most pitiless of all composers." It took "Lohengrin" no less than nine years to reach Berlin ; and the same manager who then waited so long has repeated his wise policy in the case of the "Nibelungen," which he persistently refused, until the enormous success of Neumann's performances in Berlin absolutely compelled him to change his policy. Owing to his incompetent management, none of Wagner's operas are so well rendered in Berlin as in Vienna, Munich, Leipzig, and Hamburg. And yet the official list of performances given at the Imperial Opera in Berlin during 1882–1883 begins with Wagner, to whom thirty-two nights were devoted ; the next six composers being Mozart with twenty-one, Meyerbeer eighteen, Lortzing eighteen, Bizet eighteen, Weber sixteen, Gluck eleven. The whole number of performances given was two hundred and thirty-seven, of which only twenty-four were devoted to those Italian composers whose popularity once prevented Wagner's operas from being accepted. *Tempora mutantur !*

"TRISTAN AND ISOLDE."

N strict chronologic order "Rheingold" and "Walküre," the first two dramas of the tetralogy, ought to follow "Lohengrin." Wagner interrupted the composition of the "Nibelungen" when he had finished the second act of "Siegfried," because he could only hope for the realization of his plans in the distant future, and felt the necessity of preserving some connection with theatric life by means of one or two operas complete in themselves. The result was "Tristan and Isolde" and "Die Meistersinger," which will accordingly be considered first, so as not to separate the parts of the tetralogy.

Perhaps the most regrettable circumstance in Wagner's life is the fact that for five years following the completion of "Lohengrin" he entirely abandoned composition.

"*Tristan and Isolde.*"

The first years of his exile were spent in Switzerland, where he devoted most of his time to literary work. It cannot be denied that the essays and treatises of this period, among which are "Art and Revolution," "Art and Climate," "The Art Work of the Future," "A Communication to my Friends" (autobiographic), "Opera and Drama," rank with the very best æsthetic and critical literature of all times and nations. But another opera like "Lohengrin" would have been of even greater value. There are men living who could deduce his art principles from his works almost as well as he did it himself; but no one who could write a new "Lohengrin."

The date of these theoretic treatises completely disproves the oft-repeated assertion that Wagner first reasoned out his art-principles, and then applied them to his works. Years before their appearance he had already, in the "Dutchman" and "Tannhäuser," laid the foundation of his new musical structure, the novel features of which suggested themselves to him in the heat of musical inspiration and through observation of what was most artistic and dramatic in the work of his predecessors. Even in the weaker productions of frivolous writers he acknowledges that he often discovered to his delight passages of a definiteness of melodic expression which allowed the vocalist-actor to produce an effect never equalled by an ordinary actor; while on the other hand, in the most important works he was pained to find the frivolous and commonplace side by side with what was noble and perfect. His aim was conscientiously to avoid the former and strive for the latter.

"Tristan and Isolde" is the work in which his aspirations and principles are most fully embodied. "This work," he says, "I am willing to submit to the severest tests that result from my theoretic assertions; not because I formed it in accordance with my system, — for all theory was completely forgotten by me, — but because here at last I moved about with the utmost freedom and the most absolute disregard for every theoretic consideration, in such a manner that in the course of execution I became aware that I went far beyond my system." In "Tristan" there are no repetitions of words, no distinct lyric forms and choruses, as in the earlier works. There is no melody that exists for its own sake, although the whole drama is pervaded by one long and uninterrupted flow of melody, and those who cannot hear it must be likened to the man who could not see the forest on account of the trees. What Wagner said of Beethoven applies still more to his own Tristan : "Here there is nothing that is adventitious, no framework for the melody ; but everything becomes melody, every part of the accompaniment, every rhythmic note, — yes, even the pauses."

"Every part of the accompaniment is a melody." That expresses it precisely. And the polyphonic art with which these melodies are united, intertwined, and displayed amidst ever-varying effects of orchestral illumination and coloring, is something which no previous composer had attained. What a kaleidoscope is for colors, Wagner's orchestra is for sounds. But while colors afford little besides gratification of a sense, these tones speak to the heart with the force of intense, elemental passion. Action there is little in "Tristan," except in the first act. But the essence of the drama is not action, physical movement, but the play and development of emotion. Fault has been found with the long pauses in the action, filled up with music and pantomime. But hear what Dr. Stone says about Salvini, the greatest living actor : "The individual words came about one a second, and the pauses were astonishingly long. They frequently amounted to four, several times to five, and at the great crises of the play to seven continuous seconds. And yet there was no sense of delay or of interruption, but quite the reverse." If this is true in the spoken drama, how much more in the music drama, in which the orchestra not only assumes the explanatory function of the Greek chorus, but analyzes the feelings and motives of the characters on the stage with the psychologic subtlety of a modern novelist.

"DIE MEISTERSINGER."

FTER the completion of "Tristan and Isolde," in 1859, Wagner made unsuccessful attempts to get it produced in Paris, Carlsruhe, Vienna, and elsewhere. In Vienna it was abandoned after the fifty-fourth rehearsal. Trusting in the future, he continued his labors by writing "Die Meistersinger," when suddenly, in 1864, a new and propitious star appeared on the horizon. Ludwig I. ascended the throne of Bavaria; and one of his very first acts was to despatch a special messenger, who, after considerable search, succeeded in finding Wagner, and brought him to Munich. The King presented him with a beautiful villa, and gave him not only his warmest personal regards, but almost unlimited control of his pecuniary and artistic resources. Wagner sent for Hans von Bülow, who had some years previously been induced, on hearing a performance of "Lohengrin" at Weimar, to abandon law and study music under Wagner at Zürich. Bülow prepared a version of the difficult score of "Tristan" for the piano, which Wagner himself pronounced a marvel, and which is doubtless the finest vocal score of any opera in existence. He also assisted in rehearsing and conducting "Tristan," which was produced on June 10, 1865, and made a deep impression on the audience. For a whole decade, however, the work remained confined to Munich; and up to the present day the only other cities that have heard it entire are Weimar, Berlin, Königsberg, Leipzig, Hamburg, Bremen, London, and Vienna. In the opinion of competent judges "Tristan" represents the culminating point of Wagner's genius; but its subject is so sad, the execution so difficult, and the music throughout on such a high level of passion, that it will probably never become so popular as "Lohengrin," "Walküre," and "Die Meistersinger."

This last-named opera is doubtless destined to attain as great popularity as "Lohengrin," if not greater. In Germany "Lohengrin" is at present the favorite opera. In Berlin, where it was at first neglected for nine years, it was given ten times last season, and "Die Meistersinger" only four times. But the time is not far distant when "Die Meistersinger" will rise above all other operas by the number of its performances. The score of this opera was completed in 1867. In course of eight months, sixty-six rehearsals were held at the Munich Opera, the chorister being Hans

" *Die Meistersinger.* "

Richter, who had copied the score for the press, and carefully studied it under Wagner. On June 21, 1868, the first performance was given, and lasted six hours. The audience was quite as notable as that which in 1876 heard the "Nibelungen" at Bayreuth for the first time. Bülow was conductor, and Wagner listened in the King's box. The enthusiasm was extraordinary ; and the following year the new opera began its career throughout Germany. Among the last cities to accept it were Vienna and Berlin, where the royal managers conducted themselves in such a way that Wagner came to the conclusion that their object not only was "not to give his work, but to prevent its being given at other theatres." Originally "Die Meistersinger" had been intended for Vienna ; but Wagner received an official note informing him that his name had been sufficiently considered for the present, and that it was now the turn of another composer. This "other composer" he ascertained was the great and immortal Jacques Offenbach ! It is thus that the Germans have always treated their men of genius.

"Die Meistersinger" is Wagner's only comic opera ; but not exactly in the sense in which the word comic was understood by his great rival, Offenbach, or even by Mozart, Rossini, Auber, Lortzing, Nicolai. The humor is essentially German, — a combination, always within æsthetic limits, of *naïve* playfulness, exuberant animal spirits, satire, practical jokes, burlesque, and withal an under-current of seriousness, and even sadness. Each of Wagner's operas is so novel in subject and musical ideas, that, on hearing one after the other, one might imagine himself transferred to a different planet. But the greatest differences prevail between "Tristan" and "Meistersinger," although they were composed in succession. "Tristan" is like a rapturous nocturne in the tropics ; "Die Meistersinger" like a festival day in the bracing, cheerful atmosphere of the north. So great is the difference, that the author himself called the first work a *Handlung* (action, plot) ; the second an *Opera*, as it contains choruses in abundance, lyric pieces, processions, and even a dance. This has been interpreted as a recantation of his principles ; but it is no such thing. In its general structure this work is as dramatic and Wagnerian as any ; but the subject, being historic and humorous, is so different from the others, that it naturally called for a different treatment. As Mr. F. Hueffer remarks in his charming little book on Wagner, in this opera "we find that the most striking jocular effects are frequently produced by a clever *persiflage* of certain traditional modes of expression. Beckmesser delights in long-winded roulades and fioriture, and the turns and trills of David would do credit to any Italian singing-master. Moreover, the local and historical tone pervading the whole would have been utterly destroyed if the utterances of even the elevated characters had not to some extent been made to tally with the language of their period, which was not the language of pure passion. It is thus that Wagner makes ornaments of his chains, and attains the highest freedom of poetic purpose, where he seems entangled in the meshes of conventionalism. On the other hand, he has nowhere written more truly impassioned strains where pure emotion comes into play. In addition to this, the score abounds with melodious beauties of the highest order."

37

BAYREUTH.

F Wagner could have remained in Munich, Bayreuth would never have attained its present importance for the musical world. He intended to build a splendid theatre on a new plan in the Bavarian capital, and the famous architect, Semper, had already prepared sketches for it, when the musical, clerical, and political cabals that had been formed through jealousy of Wagner's influence on the King assumed such disagreeable dimensions that he found it advisable to leave the city. The King, however, remained his friend and patron, and supplied some of the means for carrying out the colossal project of building a special theatre in an out-of-the-way town of twenty thousand inhabitants, and producing there, with the co-operation of the greatest vocalists of the time, the Nibelung tetralogy. No less than nine hundred thousand marks were wanted ; and to obtain these Carl Tausig and the Countess von Schleinitz conceived the plan of forming Wagner societies, with a membership due of $225, entitling the holder to seats for the first three festival performances to be given at Bayreuth. Thanks to the growing popularity of Wagner's operas, the plan proved successful. Societies were formed in all German and many foreign cities, and the result was the festival of 1876, at which were assembled the most notable collection of crowned heads, artists, musicians, authors, and managers probably ever brought together by any theatric performance.

No musician had ever received such homage and honors as were here showered on Wagner. What a contrast to his early Parisian days, when hunger compelled him to arrange trivial operatic melodies for the odious cornet, and even to prepare a pianoforte score of Bellini's " Puritani " ! After the innumerable trials through which his iron will had enabled him to pass without yielding an inch of his principles, it might have been expected that his countrymen would congratulate him on his triumph, which was at the same time a triumph for German music ; since previous German opera had been a mere eclectic mixture of Italian, French, and a few German elements, while here was a work thoroughly German and new in style, and constituting, moreover, a glorification of national mythology. But the majority of scribes assailed the work in the most unmeasured terms. When subsequently they had an opportunity at home to become better acquainted with it, they almost invariably revised their opinions ; and since Wagner's death the work has been quietly accepted as a classic. But its original reception by the German press will forever remain as a colossal monument to that national arrogance, folly, and prejudice, which Schopenhauer always lashed in such cutting terms.

Bayreuth itself was a special object of abuse. Why not give the tetralogy at one of the German capitals, in one of the old-established opera-houses? A sensible question, no doubt, but quite easily answered. Munich, which Wagner had to leave, was the only large city where he could have produced his tetralogy in accordance with his own intentions. Elsewhere his operas were not only condensed and mutilated, but interpreted quite in the old operatic style, so that only the lyric numbers found favor with the public, the much grander dramatic portions remaining entirely misunderstood, because misinterpreted. To facilitate comprehension, Wagner wrote masterly analyses of the "Dutchman" and "Tannhäuser," in which his genius as stage-manager is conspicuous in every line. These he distributed free among the opera-houses. Some years later, having exhausted his stock, he wrote to one of the managers for a copy; when the six copies he had sent were all found uncut and carefully locked up in the library!

In other words, if he was to have an opportunity during his lifetime to teach the singers his new style, he was obliged to appeal to his friends and build the Bayreuth theatre. There everything was in accordance with his wishes. A quiet country town, with none of a city's distractions; his own singers and players, mindful of every hint; an amphitheatric auditorium, in which the spectators could not sit in boxes and display their millinery, but were obliged to attend to the drama; perfect ventilation, and freedom from danger; no drowning of beautiful orchestral passages by ill-timed applause of solo-singers; no recalls until the end of the last act; no gesticulating conductor and scraping and blowing musicians to impede the view, but an invisible orchestra, whose sounds seemed to hover over the singers as the mingled perfumes over a bed of flowers. This was Wagner's ideal. It could not be attained by him in any German city at that time, and was for the first time realized at Bayreuth.

"THE RING OF THE NIBELUNG."

HE Nibelung's Ring consists of four dramas, — "Rheingold," fore-evening; "Die Walküre," first day; "Siegfried," second day; "Die Götterdämmerung," third day. The poetry of these dramas was written in inverse order. First came "Siegfried's Death," which is now "Götterdämmerung." The original text contained so much narrative and episodic matter, that the author decided to expand it into a new drama, "Young Siegfried." This in turn gave rise to "Die Walküre," and finally, for the same reason, to "Rheingold." The music, however, was composed in the order in which the dramas now stand. More than a quarter of a century elapsed between the time of the original conception of the work and its final completion in 1875. The rehearsals at Bayreuth were superintended from beginning to end by Wagner, who not only gave hints to the orchestra, but was continually on the stage correcting the accent, expression, gestures, attitudes, and actions of the vocalists by personal example. Between Aug. 13 and 30, 1876, the first performances were given, Wilhelmj being leading violinist, Hans Richter

39

conductor, and Frau Materna the interpreter of the dominant *rôle* of Brünnhilde. " Rheingold " and " Walküre " had been previously given at Munich, against Wagner's wishes ; but the other two dramas were for the first time heard on this occasion. Wagner wished to retain his tetralogy for exclusive performance at Bayreuth, where it was his intention to have a series of annual performances of the best German operas, and to found, in connection with this, a high school for teaching the vocal art and acting in combination. But the difficulties which stood in the way of such a plan, no less than the urgent solicitations of managers and the public, induced him to grant the " Nibelungen " permission to leave Bayreuth. The leading cities made immediate use of this permission, and the smaller towns, that did not have the resources for mounting such a work, were visited by Neumann's travelling Wagner company ; so that at the present date more than thirty cities, including London, have heard the complete tetralogy. Berlin alone decided to wait nine years, as in the case of " Lohengrin." The manager did not like the work, and concluded that it would not pay. But when Neumann's company arrived and gave, within two months, five performances of " Rheingold," fifteen of " Die Walküre," six of " Siegfried," and seven of " Die Götterdämmerung," he changed his mind, and has now purchased the privilege of producing the entire work. The comparative popularity of the four dramas is indicated by these figures, as well as by the statement of a gentleman in Berlin who had to pay a speculator for a poor seat, 2.50, 7, 4, and 5 marks, respectively, for the four evenings.

This popular verdict does not quite tally with the opinion of connoisseurs. " Rheingold," indeed, although it contains many beautiful things, has less musical value than any other work following " The Flying Dutchman." It would seem as if the five years of cessation from composition that came between " Lohengrin " and " Rheingold " had slightly dulled the edge of Wagner's imagination. In " Die Walküre " the fire of inspiration again burns brighter ; and when, in " Siegfried," he forges the sword of the Volsung, the white heat of genius is reached. As already stated in the article on " Tristan," the composition of the tetralogy was interrupted at the end of the second act of " Siegfried," and not resumed until " Tristan " and the " Meistersinger " had been completed. This period represents the most perfect spontaneity and the highest development of Wagner's genius. After hearing each of his works from five to more than twenty times, the present writer has come to the conclusion that the highest rank will be bestowed by posterity on the second act of " Tristan " and the third acts of " Meistersinger," " Siegfried," and " Götterdämmerung." From a purely musical point of view, that is to say ; from the ideal Wagnerian point of view, " Parsifal " must rank highest. In this, his latest and most mature work, is fulfilled the poet Herder's prophecy, that a man would arise to overthrow the booth of the flimsy, incoherent, operatic kling-klang, and erect an odeon, — a coherent lyric structure, in which poetry, music, action, and scenery should be one and inseparable.

"PARSIFAL."

HE creative impulse appears to have been as irresistible in Wagner as the craving for artificial stimulants in the case of many nervous people. The explanation of this phenomenon is easily found. Artistic work and the consciousness of producing an immortal composition afford the most intense pleasure of which the human mind is capable. Wagner states that during the composition of "Tannhäuser" his whole mind was so completely absorbed, that he was tortured by a great fear that he would die before its completion; and when the last notes had been written he felt as if he had escaped a great danger.' He never waited until he had finished one stage-play before he commenced another. At the time of his death he is said to have been at work on a new drama on a Buddhistic subject. The plan of "Die Meistersinger" was conceived during the "Lohengrin" period, having been originally intended as a comic sequel to "Tannhäuser," after the manner of the Greek satyr-dramas. "Siegfried's Death" occupied his thoughts at an early period in his career, and "Parsifal" was commenced before the completion of "Götterdämmerung." Indeed there is reason to believe that the original plan of "Parsifal" dates back many years. It contains features which strikingly suggest Wagner's early purpose of making "Jesus of Nazareth" the subject of a sacred drama.

When "Parsifal" was first produced at Bayreuth, in 1882, friend and foe united in wonder at the spontaneity and freshness that characterized the music written at such an advanced period of life. Yet this fact was not so remarkable as it seemed. Almost all the great masters, whether they died old or young, wrote their best work toward the end of their career. Mention need only be made of the last symphonies of Beethoven, Schubert, Haydn; the last operas of Gluck, Weber, Mozart; the last quartettes of Beethoven, etc. "Parsifal" is as original as any of its predecessors; but in one sense it may be considered a synopsis of Wagner's whole career. It curiously unites features that occur in the earlier dramas. The curse-laden *Kundry* is the female counterpart of the Flying Dutchman. As a temptress, in the second act, she assumes the *rôle* of *Venus* in "Tannhäuser." *Parsifal* is the father of *Lohengrin;* and while in the earlier opera we have only a narrative of the Holy Grail, in "Parsifal" we enter the sanctuary itself and behold the mysteries. With the "Nibelungen," "Parsifal" has in common certain philosophic teachings, and with "Tristan" it is closely connected by the sad character of the music, — which, however, has become here more serene, and less pathetic, except in the *Amfortas* scenes. In scenic beauty "Parsifal" surpasses even the tetralogy. It contains much choral music of a simple character, and a gaily weird flower-girl scene, which rivals the splendors of a Parisian ballet, and which, together with the demoniacal music of the wizard *Klingsor*, affords a striking contrast to the ecclesiastic character of the rest of the music. Those who imagined that Wagner had exhausted the possibilities of instrumental coloring were surprised to find in "Parsifal" a new fairy-land of unheard sounds, blended with such perfect art that, as in the colors of the solar spectrum, the transition from one to another is imperceptible.

Six years after the Nibelung festival, on July 26, 1882, "Parsifal" had its first performance at Bayreuth, and proved a still greater success than the tetralogy, as far as the performance was concerned. When Wagner first announced his plan of building a special theatre at Bayreuth, it was derided on all sides as the air-castle of a crazy musician. He appealed to his friends; the theatre was built, and all the world went to see it. Then the critics said : " Once the mountain has come to the prophet ; but it will not come again." " Parsifal " was finished, and the mountain again went to Bayreuth. The next war-cry was, that Wagner's magnetic personality accounted for this miracle. Wagner died ; the artists assembled and gave another series of performances at Bayreuth, no less successful both artistically and financially than the preceding series. Immediately after his death, in accordance with German traditions, Wagner was canonized, and no one permitted to say another word against him. The critics, in despair, and ashamed to confess their partial or complete conversion, now contented themselves with attacking those who had been sufficiently liberal-minded and reckless to recognize Wagner's genius while he still lived among them. Before long, however, this method of hiding their confusion will strike even them as comic, and they will want a new motto. They might say that everybody now goes to hear Wagner because it is "the fashion." That would be exceedingly sarcastic, and at the same time quite true. As a rule, of course, people and things become fashionable suddenly, while Wagner required more than thirty years to attain that result. But he clearly forms the exception which only proves the rule. His only aim, as everybody knows, was to win ephemeral applause ; and he spent his whole life in pandering to the depraved taste of the operatic public. In " Rienzi " he still aimed at artistic results ; but in all the other operas he wrote absurd librettos, arias for showing off the singers, dry recitatives for giving people an opportunity to talk, overlooked the symphonic capabilities of the orchestra, and made the singers execute so many runs and trills that they had no opportunity to act or to pronounce their words distinctly. What will be the result ? In five hundred years this fashionable craze will subside, and all of Wagner's operas be consigned to oblivion, — with the exception, perhaps, of " The Flying Dutchman," " Tannhäuser," " Lohengrin," " Tristan," " Meistersinger," " The Nibelung's Ring," and " Parsifal."

MR. THEODORE THOMAS.

A N impartial regard for everything that is good in music, no matter whether it is old or new, German, French, Italian, or English, has always been a notable trait of Mr. Theodore Thomas's character. Like other musicians, he doubtless has his likes and dislikes; but this does not prevent him from bestowing equal care and labor on everything that appeals to a refined and healthful taste, so that it is not easy to tell from his programmes whether he belongs to the conservative or the advanced school. Prominent German conductors are generally distinguished for their fine interpretation of the works of a special epoch or composer; but Mr. Thomas conducts a Bach fugue, a Mozart symphony, a Strauss waltz, a Handel oratorio, or a selection from Wagner's "Götterdämmerung" with the same technical finish and the same sympathetic realization of the composer's intentions.

When he first commenced his orchestral concerts his aim was to familiarize the public with the best music of the classical period, while at the same time introducing the works of contemporary musicians, — of Berlioz, Liszt, Rubinstein, Raff, Saint-Saëns, and especially Wagner. Year after year he pursued the policy of hardly ever giving a concert without at least one Wagnerian selection. At first people shook their heads when they heard this music, so full of modulations and discords, so devoid of cadences and the usual rhythmic divisions. But the orchestra was so well trained, and the striking motives and glowing colors of these complicated scores were placed in such a favorable light, that gradually *ennui* and indifference were followed by interest, and this again by enthusiasm. At the great festival in New York two years ago, when Mr. Thomas conducted an orchestra of three hundred musicians, while Frau Materna interpreted her famous *rôle* of Brünnhilde, it was universally admitted that this was not only the climax of the festival, but the grandest concert ever given in America. It reminded one of what the Emperor William said after a performance in Wagner's theatre at Bayreuth: "You see now what a great general can do with his army."

The Kaiser's comparison of a conductor with a general is very appropriate. When an officer parades his army, the spectators admire the promptness with which every

Mr. Theodore Thomas.

command is heeded, and the uniformity and precision of every movement; but if they will pay a visit to the barracks they will see what an infinite amount of trouble is involved in the process of training the raw recruits. Many who see a conductor gracefully beating the air at a concert with his *báton*, think they could do that just as easily themselves. They might as well attempt to play a Chopin concerto the first time they touch a piano. The conductor has to know every part of the score, and follow each instrument, ready to give a hint when it is needed.

Some conductors indulge in a vast amount of excited gesticulation; but this is a mistake. A conductor should conceal the difficulties of his task as carefully as a performer. To show them is to destroy the illusion, as in the case of an actor who laughs at his own jokes. Mr. Thomas is the least demonstrative and most graceful of conductors. He does his work before he comes to the concert-hall, so that when he takes his place at the stand the least nod of the head, movement of the left hand, or raising of the eyelids, has an electric effect. And woe to the musician who does not heed these hints! Personally Mr. Thomas is the most genial and amiable of men; but in the battle-field he is stern and severe, like any other general. His aim is to give not only good music, but perfect performances; and these he is bound to have, at the risk of any pecuniary loss or personal friction.

Mr. Thomas is one of the busiest men in the United States. The fact that last summer he gave seventy-four concerts within as many days, extending from the Atlantic to the Pacific, will give an idea of his labors. Every concert brings with it its own anxiety for success; and this, combined with the task of arranging an immense number of programmes, always with an eye to artistic perspective, and with the constant travel by day and night, calls for an iron constitution. He is now in the best period of his manhood, having been born Oct. 11, 1835, in Ostfriesland. In 1845 the family came to America, where Theodore made his appearance in New York as solo violinist at concerts. During the engagements of Jenny Lind, Sontag, Grisi, and Mario, he was a leading violinist in the orchestra, and subsequently became conductor of several Italian and German opera companies. In 1854 the famous Mason-Thomas chamber-concerts were commenced, which became the germ of the later orchestral concerts. In 1864–1865 the first series of symphony concerts was given. In 1877–1878 he was conductor of the New York Philharmonic Society, and after an absence of one year at Cincinnati, as director of the College of Music, was unanimously re-elected by the Society. Of the Brooklyn Philharmonic Society he first became conductor in 1863, and has held that position almost continuously to the present day. The various concert tours throughout the country need not be referred to in detail. They have been of inestimable value in developing musical taste and intelligence. The most successful was that of last summer, under the management of Mr. Charles E. Locke.

Mr. Thomas has thus been in turn concert-soloist, orchestral player, operatic conductor, chamber-music player, and orchestral conductor. To all these positions he added, a few years ago, that of chorus-conductor by founding the New York Chorus Society, which is already one of the best organizations in the country, and has given such difficult works as Schumann's "Faust," Gounod's "Redemption," and scenes from "Parsifal," with a technical finish and intelligence that reflected equal credit on the Society and the conductor.

FRAU AMALIA MATERNA.

RAU AMALIA FRIEDRICH MATERNA needs no introduction to the American people. She now visits this country
for the second time, and her name is known wherever the art
of dramatic singing is valued. In coming centuries people
will read of her as the artist who first impersonated two
of Wagner's greatest female characters, in accordance with
his own suggestions and directions. In connection with
Schröder-Devrient, Schnorr von Carolsfeld, Niemann, Vogel,
Winkelmann, Scaria, and others, she will be remembered as
one of the band of singers who helped to form and interpret a
new style of vocal music, neither florid nor lyric, but half-way
between impassioned declamation and rhythmic melody.

She was born on July 10, 1847, in a small Austrian town,
and received her first musical instruction from her father, a school-teacher. She
learned with ease the arias in Haydn's and Mozart's Masses, and at the age of
twelve was placed in a music-school at Graz. A year later she appeared in a
performance of " Lohengrin " as *Ortrud,* — one of the *rôles* on which her subsequent reputation was first based. The death of her father prevented her from
continuing her studies, but she subsequently found an asylum in the house of one
of her brothers, and on her return to Graz was engaged as soloist at three churches,
and often heard at concerts.

In 1864 a new theatre was opened, and Materna engaged as leading singer, her
first venture being in Suppé's " Flotte Bursche." Here she remained two years, singing
the *rôles* of Suppé's and Offenbach's heroines. As *Belle Hélène,* she appeared no less
than one hundred and thirty times. In 1866 she married the well-known actor, Carl
Friedrich, and henceforth lived in Vienna, where she continued as operetta singer for
some time. Some of her admirers having expressed the opinion that she was qualified
to appear in grand opera, she began to study under Proch, and was engaged by Dingel-
stedt for a series of preliminary performances, which proved so successful that she was
engaged at the Imperial Opera-House as soon as her contract at the Carl Theater expired. Her first *rôles* were in " L'Africaine," " Ballo in Maschera," " Fidelio," " Don
Juan." To these *rôles* she subsequently added others in " Les Huguenots," " Armida,"
" Prophète," " Aida," " Medea," " Euryanthe," " Idomeneo," " Queen of Sheba," etc.

But her greatest triumphs were celebrated in the Wagnerian *rôles* of *Ortrud,
Elisabeth, Venus; Adriano, Brünnhilde, Kundry, Isolde.* Wagner first heard of
her through Scaria, in 1874, after both these singers had assisted at a private performance of an act from " Die Walküre," in Vienna. He expressed a desire to see
her, and she visited him at Bayreuth, on her way home from London. She sang
" Dich theure Halle," from " Tannhäuser ; " and he was so much pleased with her voice,
style, and whole appearance, so eminently adapted to the *rôle* of *Brünnhilde,* that he
at once engaged her for the first Bayreuth festival ; and, however much opinions
differed in regard to the tetralogy, in one point friend and enemy were agreed, — that

Materna's *Brünnhilde* was one of the greatest operatic achievements on record, — a revelation of a new style of dramatic vocalism, and at the same time an exhibition of histrionic talent which some of the most famous actresses might envy. How well Wagner was pleased with her performance was shown by the fact that at the "Parsifal" festival he again chose her to "create" the principal female *rôle*.

Frau Materna does not, and cannot, sing florid music ; she does something much nobler. She interprets the music of the greatest masters precisely as they wish it to be interpreted, merging her individuality so completely in that of the art-work, that one mistakes fiction for reality. Her voice is uncommonly rich, full, sonorous, and powerful, so that she is at her best in highly dramatic situations, where a voice like Patti's is completely drowned in the ocean of orchestral sound.

———•———

HERR SCARIA AND HERR WINKELMANN.

ERR EMIL SCARIA was born, Sept. 18, 1840, at Graz. He is, therefore, like Frau Materna, a native of Austria, — the country in which music unites German richness and nobility with Italian grace and beauty and Hungarian vivacity. Law was his chosen study, but was subsequently abandoned in favor of music. He had just left the music-school at Graz when Frau Materna was admitted. On April 14, 1860, he made his *début* at Pesth, in "Les Huguenots." Two years later he went to London, and continued his studies under Garcia. Successive engagements at Dessau, Leipzig, and Dresden followed, until 1872, when he was engaged at the Imperial Opera in Vienna, where he has been ever since. Herr Scaria is doubtless the greatest living basso. He is equally famous in tragic and comic *rôles*. Among his greatest parts are the *Flying Dutchman* ; *Hans Sachs*, in "Die Meistersinger ; " *Wotan* in the "Nibelungen," and *Gurnemanz* in "Parsifal." In this latter part indeed, he attracted as much admiring attention at the second Bayreuth festival as Frau Materna's *Brünnhilde* did at the first. His noble, manly, rich, and sonorous tones went to the heart of every spectator, while his enunciation was so distinct that not one word of the text was lost ; and at the same time his acting was intelligent, impressive, and finished in every detail. Herr Scaria is an intimate friend of Bismarck, at whose house he is frequently seen as a guest ; and witnesses state that he has succeeded with his song in moving the "man of iron," — a true modern Orpheus.

Herr Hermann Winkelmann became, about a year ago, the third in the great trio of Wagnerian singers at Vienna. His gifts were first appreciated at their full value by Manager Pollini, of the Hamburg Stadt-theater, who engaged him for five years.

Herr Scaria and Herr Winkelmann.

Here his fame as an interpreter of Wagner spread so rapidly that tempting offers were made him from various sides. He accepted that made by Herr Jahn, of the Vienna Imperial Opera. Vienna is the centre of European musical life at present, and no expense is spared by the management to secure the best singers and a varied repertory. As soon as Winkelmann's contract at Hamburg had expired, he went to Vienna, where preparations were at once made to carry out a project often deferred for want of a suitable dramatic tenor. Wagner's "Tristan and Isolde" was produced for the first time in the Austrian capital; and thanks to the efforts of Materna, Winkelmann, and Scaria, and Hans Richter's admirable orchestra, this drama at once assumed the rank of a regular *répertoire* opera. Twenty-three years ago Wagner attempted to produce "Tristan" at Vienna; but after fifty-four rehearsals, the task was abandoned as impossible, the principal singers having declared that by the time they had memorized one act, they had again forgotten the others. This fact shows how much vocalists have strengthened not only their voices, but their memory and intelligence, under the influence of Wagner's music. Herr Winkelmann sings all the tenor *rôles* of Wagner without a prompter; and the extent of his repertory was concisely indicated in the despatch which he sent to Mr. Thomas, in reply to a question: "I sing all classical arias, and everything by Wagner."

His greatest achievement was at the second Bayreuth festival, where he "created" the *rôle* of *Parsifal*. There were three sets of singers, and among those who sang on the first night were Materna, Winkelmann, and Scaria. This first-night cast was also known as the "Sunday cast," because they sang every Sunday, — when there was always the largest attendance, because the Germans consider true and refined art to be as sacred as religion. Like his two colleagues, Herr Winkelmann is an excellent actor; and the only thing to be regretted is that, like Wagner's music, these three artists can only be judged during their present visit from one point of view. Herr Winkelmann was born at Brunswick in 1849. His father at first opposed his plan of going on the stage, as he wished him to take charge of his pianoforte manufactory. But the histrionic impulse in the young man was too strong to be resisted, and so he studied the vocal art at Hanover and Paris, making his first appearance in opera at Sondershausen. His popularity in Germany is well shown by the fact that every time he has signed a contract at one city for several years, a manager has appeared from another city, and agreed to pay a heavy forfeit in order to secure him at once. At Vienna he was immediately engaged for ten years after his *début* as *Guest*.

MADAME CHRISTINE NILSSON.

CHRISTINE NILSSON, like Jenny Lind, was born in Sweden twenty-three years after the original "Swedish Nightingale," and the same year as Adelina Patti, — Aug. 20, 1843. She was the eighth child of a peasant who, besides cultivating the soil, was the principal singer in the Lutheran church of the village, and who gave Christine her first music-lessons. Her brother Carl was a popular violinist, who first discovered his sister's talent for singing, and took her along when he played at fairs and weddings. Here she sang those simple, expressive Scandinavian folk-songs which still constitute one of the most attractive features of her concert repertory. At one of these fairs an art-loving lawyer from the metropolis, Dr. Tornechjelm, heard her, and was so much impressed with her singing, appearance, and demeanor, that he begged her parents for permission to provide for her musical education. She spent two years in a seminary at Gothenburg; and then, having gained the reluctant consent of her parents, went to Paris, where she studied three years under François Wartel. In the *rôle* of *Violetta* she made her first *début*, at the Théâtre Lyrique, in 1864; her second *rôle* being the *Queen of Night* in "The Magic Flute." Four years later she was engaged at the Grand Opéra, where she created the part of *Ophelia* in Ambroise Thomas's "Hamlet," and aroused extraordinary enthusiasm. England and other countries were now visited, and everywhere she was hailed as the new Swedish nightingale, and the equal of Patti. Her first American tour was made, in 1870, under Mr. Strakosch; her second in 1873.

As a singer Mme. Nilsson occupies a position midway between the ultra-lyric style of Mme. Patti and the ultra-dramatic style of Frau Materna. She combines in the happiest manner some of the best qualities of each style, — the florid and the emotional. Her best parts are the leading female *rôles* in "Mignon," "Faust," "Hamlet," "Lohengrin," "Mefistofele," "Huguenots," "Tell," "Don Giovanni," etc., in each of which her conception is as original as it is attractive. She avoids exaggeration; and the strongest outbursts of passion, which transgress the line of beauty, are foreign to her nature. But the tone of her voice naturally has a tinge of passion, and thus everything she sings is imbued with feeling. The range of her voice was formerly nearly three octaves; but, in accordance with Rossini's advice, she has lately made sparing use of the highest part. She also plays the violin, and even her whistling is said to have a unique charm. In 1872 she was married at Westminster Abbey to M. Auguste Rouzand, of Paris.

The well-known Viennese critic, Dr. Hanslick, says of Mme. Nilsson's voice: " Her intonation is always so exquisitely pure that we should suspect her of being a good violinist, if we did not happen to know that she is one. As to her intonation, so we always listen to her pronunciation, which, both in French and Italian, is a model of correctness and distinctness."

I. TANNHÄUSER.

(a) OVERTURE, BACCHANALE, CHORUS OF SIRENS.

NO concert-piece is better known or more admired than the overture to "Tannhäuser." It is, as Liszt remarks, a complete symphonic work, — " a poem 'on the same subject as the opera, and equally comprehensive." It depicts the struggle between good and evil, virtue and sin ; on the one side the solemn religious strains of the Pilgrims' chorus, on the other, the seductive chorus of Sirens and the wild shouts of Bacchanalian revelry. The religious motive appears first, but is gradually submerged in the rising tide of sensual sounds. The Venus motive, assigned to the violins, continues with thrilling, terrible persistence, when suddenly the tide changes, the religious element predominates, and gradually reaches a climax in the final hymn of triumph. An extremely interesting episode of musical history is connected with the *bacchanale* which follows the overture. When, in accordance with an Imperial order, "Tannhäuser" was accepted for performance at the Grand Opera in Paris in 1861, Wagner was given to understand that he must introduce a ballet in the second act for the benefit of the highlife subscribers, who dined late, and insisted on having a ballet after their arrival in the theatre. Wagner refused absolutely to mar the artistic unity of his work by any such procedure ; but undertook to enlarge the scene at the opening of the first act in the grotto of Venus, and give it the character of musical and terpsichorean revelry. The result is the most dissonant musical orgy ever written, — a piece that is apt to be caviare to the public, but is highly relished by epicures. Wagner had to pay the penalty of his stubborn devotion to art-principles. The Jockey Club took their revenge by hissing the opera, and making such a noise with whistles that the music could hardly be heard ; and the result was that fiasco which subsequently led

"ELISABETH, MAY I NOT ESCORT THEE?"

(Tannhäuser.)

to Wagner's supposed retaliation in his burlesque on the siege of Paris, and to the long-continued enmity of the French chauvinists to the "Prussian" Wagner, — who was born in Saxony !

(*b*) I., II., III. SCENES OF ACT II. — March and Chorus.

After *Tannhäuser*, the knightly singer, has become tired of the pleasures spread before him by *Venus* in her abode within the mountain, he returns to the scenes of his earlier life. In the hall of the Singers he meets *Elisabeth*, who expresses her pleasure at his return, and confesses her affection with that frankness which characterizes all of Wagner's heroines. The situation is described in the following extract from the textbook. The march and chorus follow as an introduction to the tournament of song, at which *Tannhäuser*, in a moment of delirious excitement, gives an account of his sinful experiences, which subsequently the Pope refuses to pardon, when the knight is redeemed through the self-sacrificing love of *Elisabeth*.

ACT II.

PRELUDE AND SCENE I.

(The Curtain rises.)

SCENE. — The Hall of Minstrels in the Wartburg; at the Back an open Prospect of the Valley.

ELISABETH

(enters in joyous emotion).

O hall of song, I give thee greeting !
　All hail to thee, thou hallowed place !
'T was here that dream, so sweet and fleeting,
　Upon my heart his song did trace.
　　But since by him forsaken,
　　A desert thou dost seem !
　　Thy echoes only waken
　　Remembrance of a dream !
But now the flame of hope is lighted,
　Thy vault shall ring with glorious war ;
For he whose strains my soul delighted,
　No longer roams afar !
Yes, now the flame of hope is lighted,
　Thy vault shall ring with glorious war ;
For he whose strains my soul delighted,
　From me no longer roams afar !

All hail to thee, all hail to thee !
Thou hall of glory dear to my heart !
Dear to my heart !
Thou hall of glory dear to my heart !

TANNHÄUSER, conducted by WOLFRAM, enters by a staircase at the back.

SCENE II.

WOLFRAM

(to TANNHÄUSER).

(He remains at the back leaning against a mural projection.)

Behold her ! Nought your meeting shall disturb.

TANNHÄUSER.

(throws himself impetuously at ELISABETH's feet).

O Princess !

51

ELISABETH

(in timid confusion).

Heav'n! do not kneel! Leave me!
Here thus we should not meet.

(She is about to depart.)

TANNHÄUSER.

We may! Oh stay!
And let me kneel forever here!

ELISABETH.

I pray thee, rise! 'T is not for thee to kneel
where thou hast conquered; this hall is thy
domain.
Rise, I implore! Thanks be to Heav'n that thou
return'st to us!
So long, where hast thou tarried?

TANNHÄUSER

(slowly rising).

Far away, in strange and distant regions; and
between yesterday and to-day Oblivion's veil
hath fallen.
Ev'ry remembran.... th forever vanish'd,
Save one thing o.... ing from the darkness;
that I then dare.... t hope
I should behold thee, nor ever raise my eyes to
thy perfection.

ELISABETH.

How wert thou led now to return to us?

TANNHÄUSER.

A marvel 't was by Heaven wrought within my
spirit!

ELISABETH

(with joyous exclamation).

I praise the Power that wrought it from out my
heart's recesses!

(Restraining herself, confused.)

Forgive, I scarcely know what I am saying!
Thy presence here, a vision doth it seem!
Strange dream of life, mysterious and alluring!
The world to me is changed.
Canst thou declare what this emotion to my
heart betokens?
In minstrels' lays delighting, I marked and lis-
tened long and oft;
Their subtle sweet inditing, to me seemed dalli-
ance soft.
But now the past to me is darken'd,
Repose and joy from me have flown!
Since fondly to thy lays I hearken'd,
The pangs of bliss and woe I 've known.

Emotions that I comprehend not,
And longings never guessed before!
Upon my bidding they depend not,
Fled are all delights of yore!
And when this land thou hadst forsaken,
Repose and joy from me had fled,
No minstrel could my heart awaken,
To me their lays seem'd sad and dead.
In slumber oft near broken-hearted;
Awake, each pain fondly recalled —
All joy had from my life departed —
Henry, Henry! Why thus am I enthrall'd?

TANNHÄUSER

(with exultation).

All praise to Love for this fair token! Love
touch'd my harp with magic sweet;
Love through my song to thee hath spoken, and
captive leads me at thy feet.

TANNHÄUSER and ELISABETH.

O blessed hour of meeting, O blessed power of
love!
At last I give thee greeting, no longer wilt thou
rove!
Now life, renewed, awaketh the hope that once
was mine!
Yes, the hope that was mine!
The cloud of sorrow breaketh; I know but joy
divine,
I know but joy divine!

WOLFRAM

(at the back).

All hope my heart forsaketh, ne'er will her heart
be mine!

TANNHÄUSER parts from ELISABETH, hastens towards
WOLFRAM, embraces him impetuously, and disappears
with him by the staircase.

ELISABETH looks after TANNHÄUSER from the balcony.

———◆———

SCENE III.

ELISABETH and the LANDGRAVE.

Enter the LANDGRAVE from a side entrance. ELISABETH
hastens to meet him, and hides her face in his breast.

LANDGRAVE.

Com'st thou at last to grace the contest, wilt
thou shun these walls no longer?
What had lured thee from thy solitude to come
amongst us?

Die Walküre.

ELISABETH.

My sov'reign, O my more than father!
Wilt thou then at last reveal to me thy secret?
Tell it I cannot; read my eyes and know.

LANDGRAVE.

This day it still shall be unspoken,
  Thy treasur'd thought thou need'st not own;
The spell shall yet remain unbroken,
  Till what the future brings is known,
  Till what the future brings is known.
So be 't. The wondrous flame that song hath
  kindled, this day shall brightly soar;
Thy joy, all hearts rejoicing, shall on this day be
  crowned.
What hath been sung shall spring to life for
  thee!

This day will see our nobles assembled; to grace
the solemn feast they now approach.
None will be absent, since they know that once
again thy hand the victor's wreath bestows.

SCENE IV.

The LANDGRAVE and ELISABETH watch the arrival of the
Guests from the balcony. Four noble Pages enter and
announce them. The LANDGRAVE directs their reception, etc.

CHORUS of KNIGHTS and NOBLES.

Hail, bright abode, where song the heart rejoices!
May lays of peace within thee never fail;
Long may we cry with loyal voices,
Prince of Thuringia, Landgrave, Hermann, hail!

II. DIE WALKÜRE. — ACT III.

  (a) RIDE OF THE WALKYRIES.
  (b) WOTAN'S FAREWELL.
  (c) MAGIC FIRE SCENE.

BRÜNNHILDE is the favorite daughter of *Wotan*, the Jupiter of Northern mythology. She is one of the Walkyries, or half-human warrior-maidens who preside over battles and convey the bodies of fallen heroes to Walhalla, the abode of the gods. *Brünnhilde* has received orders from *Wotan* not to interfere in a mortal combat between *Siegmund* and *Hunding*. But she does interfere, nevertheless, and then seeks to escape *Wotan's* vengeance. At the beginning of the third act the scene represents the top of a rocky height. On the right a fir-wood bounds the scene. On the left the entrance to a rocky cavern, which forms a natural hall; above it the rock climbs to its highest point. Towards the back the prospect is quite open; rocks of greater and less height form the border of the precipice, which slopes steeply down to the background. Detached clouds, as if driven by a storm, sweep past the rocky edge. Eight Walkyries, on horseback, appear amid the clouds. Subsequently they are joined by *Brünnhilde*, and then by *Wotan* in pursuit of her. The appropriateness of the music to the wild opening scene need not be pointed out. For disobeying his orders, *Wotan* punishes *Brünnhilde* by making her fall into a magnetic sleep on the top of the mountain. But as, in interfering in the combat, she had really followed his secret wishes (frustrated by his wife's command), he mitigates the sentence by surrounding her with a sea of flame, so that no one shall dare touch her except the hero who has sufficient courage to pass through the flames and wake her.

Die Walküre.

WOTAN

(looks with emotion into her eyes, and lifts her up).

Farewell, thou choice
unwavering child !
Thou holy pastime
and pride of my heart !
Farewell ! Farewell ! Farewell !
Must I forsake thee,
and may I sweetly
no more give thee my greeting ;
must we guide not again
our horses together ;
must my cup by another be handed ;
after our love
O am I to leave thee,
thou laughing delight of my eyes ? —
A buoyanter beacon
shall burn for thy bridal
than ever has blazed for a bride !
To fringe the rock
a flame I will raise ;
with withering clasp
it shall wait for the coward ;
the falterer fly
from Brünnhilde's fence !
To gain her is given but one,
who is freer than I, the god !

BRÜNNHILDE, with emotion and transport, throws herself
into his arms.

On the lighting pair of thy eyes, —
that lay so oft at my lips,
when for flash of coming
fight I kissed them,
when in sounds of childhood
the song that cheered
the heroes swelled from thy heart ;
on the steadfast pair of thy eyes, —
that so oft were stars of my storm,
when hope was fierce
in my heart like fire,
when world's-delightwards
my will was lifted

from dread wildering darkness, —
for latest healing
here I must lean
in last farewell
of lingering lips !
The happier man
to meet them be hailed !
On the luckless god
they gaze no longer to light him !
For so — goes
the god from thy side ;
so weans he thy godhood away.

He kisses her on both eyes, which immediately shut and
remain closed ; she sinks softly, as if weary, back into his
arms. He carries her and lays her tenderly on a low
mound of moss, over which stretches a wide-branched fir.
He once more looks at her face, and then shuts fast her
helmet ; then again his look lingers sadly on her figure,
which he at last covers with the long steel shield of the
Walkyrie. He then walks with solemn resolution into the
middle of the stage, and turns the point of his spear
towards a large mass of rock.

Loge, hear !
Hitherward listen !
As I found thee at first —
in arrowy flame,
as thereafter thou fleddest —
in fluttering fire ;
as I dealt with thee once,
I wield thee to-day !
Arise, billowing blaze,
and fold in thy fire the rock !
Loge ! Loge ! Aloft !

At the last call he strikes three times with his spear on
the stone, whereupon a flame starts out of it, which quickly
spreads into a sea of fire, to which WOTAN points out with
his spear the rim of the rock for its flow.

Who fears the spike
of my spear to face,
he will pierce not the planted fire !

He disappears in the fire towards the background.

The Curtain falls.

[ALFRED FORMAN's *Translation.*]

54

III. SIEGFRIED.—Act III.

SIEGFRIED'S WOOING.

HE third act of "Siegfried" is the natural sequel of the third act of "Die Walküre." In the first two acts of "Siegfried," we behold that hero in his forest home, where he forges the sword with which he slays the dragon. Having tasted the dragon's blood accidentally, he suddenly becomes able to understand the language of the birds, which tell him of *Brünnhilde*, the fair maiden who slumbers on the fire-guarded rock. He follows the guidance of one of the birds, cuts through the spear of *Wotan*, who endeavors to stop him, and penetrates the flames. On the top of the rock he beholds the sleeping Walkyrie covered with her shield. He removes the armor, and *Brünnhilde* lies before him in soft womanly garments. She is the first woman he has ever seen. He kneels down and kisses her long and fervently. He then starts up in alarm; *Brünnhilde* has opened her eyes. He looks at her in wonder. Both remain for some time lost in the sight of each other.

BRÜNNHILDE

(slowly and solemnly rising to a sitting posture).

Sun, I hail thee!
Hail thee, light!
Hail thee, slumberless day!
Deep was my sleep;
its dreams are done;
warn me what hero
wakens me here?

SIEGFRIED

(solemnly struck by her look and voice).

I have fought the fire
of thy flaming height;
I unfastened thy holding helm;
Siegfried was it
who woke thee so.

BRÜNNHILDE

(sitting fully up).

Gods, I hail you!
Hail thee, world!
Hail thee, earth in thy heaven!
At last my slumber swerves;
my sight leads me;
Siegfried is it,
who ends my sleep!

SIEGFRIED

(in loftiest transport).

The mother hail,
who made me a man;
earth, who fed
and fostered me on,
till here I lit on the look,
that laughs my heart from its harm!

BRÜNNHILDE

(with greatest emotion).

The mother hail,
who made thee a man;
earth, who fed
and fostered thee on;
for thy look only I lay,
to other would not awake! —

O Siegfried! Happy
hero to see!
Thou lifter of life!
Thou mastering light!
O wealth of the world, behold
how I have loved thee long!
Thou wert my sorrow,
and song as well!
I gave thee

SIEGFRIED AND MIME.

Siegfried

unbegotten my guard ;
    unborn — in its shelter
    bound thee my shield;
such was my love for thee, Siegfried !

SIEGFRIED

(softly and shyly).

So slept my mother merely ?
Left a little her son ?

BRÜNNHILDE

(smiling).

Thou capturing child!
Thou wilt come no more on thy mother. —
    Thyself am I,
soon as thy love thou hast owned.
    What thou not knowest
    know I for thee ;
    and light is lent me,
because only I love thee. —

    O Siegfried ! Siegfried!
    Wakening sun !
    I loved thee always ;
    for I alone
of Wotan's aim was a witness ;
    that I dared not to know
    by the name he dealt it;
    that I might not fathom
    and merely could feel ;
    for which I faced
    warfare and work;
    for which I thwarted
    him who had thought it ;
    for which I suffered
    shackles of sleep,
    when I failed to think it,
    and only felt ;
    since to me wholly —
    so must thou see it ! —
like love for thee, Siegfried, it looked !

SIEGFRIED.

A wonder sounds
    its word in thy song ;
but dark I deem it of sense.
    Below thy lids
    I behold the light ;
    with the wind thy breath
    has blown, I am warm,
    that thy tongue is sweet
    of sound I can tell ;
but what thou say'st in thy song
hides from my wildered heed.
    The farness but dimly
    dawns in my fancy,
    while all my senses
can see and seize on thee only. —

The clasping dread
    clings like a dream ;
    no fear I felt
    till I came to thy face.
    Unfix my manhood
    from might of thy fetters ;
give it to freedom again !

BRÜNNHILDE

(keeps him gently off, and turns her look towards the wood).

    — At hand is Grane,
    my happy horse ;
    how sweetly he browses,
    who by me slept,
for Siegfried awoke him as well.

SIEGFRIED.

My look on thy lips
    its hunger has lightened ;
    with fathomless thirst
    my mouth is on fire,
till the food of my eyes shall have fed it.

BRÜNNHILDE

(pointing with her hand).

    — And here is my shield,
    that sheltered heroes;
    the helm that held
    in its midst my head;
it helps and hides me no more !

SIEGFRIED.

I was harmed by a happy
    maid to the heart ;
    hurts from a woman
    heaped on my head ; —
I shared not in helm or shield !

BRÜNNHILDE

(with increased sadness).

Now meets me the streaming
    steel of my mail ;
    a shearing sword
    sundered its seams ;
    from the limbs of the maid
    it is loosened and lost ; —
to the last I am stripped of my strength,
and am left a woman of woe !

SIEGFRIED.

Through towering fire
    I trod to thy face ;
    my bosom of harboring
    harness was bare ;
    deeply my breast
    is drenched with the blazes;

57

to flowering flame
my blood they have flushed;
it bites with withering
wounds in my body;
the heat, that branded
Brünnhilde's height,
has burnt me here to the bone! —
Thou woman, slacken its surge!
Weaken its maddening might!

He impetuously embraces her; she leaps up, holds him off with the strength of extremest dread, and flies to the other side.

BRÜNNHILDE.

No god's grasp have I met;
the heroes meetly
hailed me as maiden;
holy went I from Walhall! —
Woe! Woe!
Woe for the sheer
unwavering shame!
Who wakes the maid,
he wounds her as well!
He has broken harness and helm;
Brünnhild' no further is found!

SIEGFRIED.

Unmoved I deem
the maid from her dreams;
Brünnhilde's sleep
soundly abides.
A woman awaken to be!

BRÜNNHILDE.

My senses unsettle!
My knowledge sinks;
wanes from me now my wisdom?

SIEGFRIED.

What made thee sing
thy wisdom meant
the light of thy love to me?

BRÜNNHILDE.

Drearily loses
my look the day;
my sight is listless,
no light I see;
deep is the night;
a snake from the dark
dreadly is sent
to seethe and surge!
Horror hisses
and hurls up its head!

She vehemently covers her eyes with her hands.

SIEGFRIED

(softly loosens her hands from her eyes).
Night befalls
the eyes that are fastened;
with the fetters, dwindles
the fitful dread;
dawn from thy darkness and see
broad is the blaze of the sun!

BRÜNNHILDE

(in greatest distress).

Sun, that swells
high for the sight of my harm! —

O Siegfried! Siegfried!
Hear me beseech!
Always was I,
always would be,
haunted with hope's
hungering sweetness —
and always to save thy ill! —

O Siegfried! Lightener!
World's delight!
Life of the earth,
and laughing lord!
Leave, ah, leave,
leave me unlost!
Force on me not
thy fiery nearness!
Shiver me not
with thy shattering will,
and lay me not waste in my love! —

Struck thee thy face
in the staying stream?
Stirred thee not sweetly the sight?
Once, if thou startle
the water to waves,
the floor of the flood
is broken and fled;
thy face falters and fades
in the blinding beat of its breast.
So leave it unwronged,
wreck not my rest;
let thyself —
seen in me so —
a glad and gladdening hero
hail thee on without end! —
O Siegfried! Siegfried!
Lightening lad!
Love — thyself,
and loose from my side;
O end not what is thy own!

SIEGFRIED.

I — love thee;
O love me no less!

58

Siegfried.

No more am I mine;
be given to me!—
A freshening water
fills and flows;
with soul and senses
all that I see
is the bounding bountiful billow;
what if my likeness
is lost in the whirl?
Myself in the flood
I fling like a fire!
I spring from my spot!
I startle the stream!
O beat me with billows!
O swallow me sweetly!
My want shall sink in thy waves!—
Awaken, Brünnhilde!
Waken, thou maid!
Live to me! Laugh to me,
sweetest delight!
Be mine! be mine! be mine!

BRÜNNHILDE.

O Siegfried, when
was I not so?

SIEGFRIED.

Such as thou hast been
be to me here!

BRÜNNHILDE.

Thine only
I always will be!

SIEGFRIED.

All that thou wilt be
show me at once!
When I have felt
and folded thee fast;
beaten my heart
home at thy bosom;
blazed in thy glance
and gathered thy breath—
eye on eye—
mouth in mouth—
then mine thou art,
as always thou wilt be and wast!
But doubt is undaunted and deep,
till Brünnhilde burns like a bride!

He has embraced her.

BRÜNNHILDE.

Till Brünnhild' burns?—

Gone is my godly
rest and forgotten;

my faltering star
thunders with fire;
wisdom is caught
and whirled in a wind;
love with his laughter
strikes it like storm!—

Till Brünnhild' burns?

O Siegfried! Siegfried!
Where is thy sight?
With the blaze of my eyes
why art thou not blind?
Where my arm is set,
unseared is thy side?
Where my blood in its storm to thee
boundlessly streams,
the wasting fire
wilt thou not feel?
Failest thou fully,
Siegfried, to fear,
the mad mastering maid?

SIEGFRIED.

Ha!—
Now our hearts are hot on each other;
now our looks with answers are lighted;
now our arms are hurt as they hold us—
meets me again
my manful mood,
and the fear, alas!
I had failed to learn—
the fear thou had'st half
helped me to feel—
I find—like a fool—
I again have fully forgotten!

With the last words he involuntarily lets BRÜNNHILDE go.

BRÜNNHILDE

(wildly laughing aloud in highest exultation of love).

O lordliest boy!
O lad without better!
Of highest deeds
thou heedless haunt!
Laughter leads me to love thee;
laughter lights me to blindness;
laughter we both will be lost in—
laughter shall fill our fall!—

Away, Walhall's
lightening world!
In dust with thy teeming
towers be down!
Farewell, greatness
and gift of gods!
End in bliss,
thou unwithering breed!
You Norns, unravel
the rope of runes!

Siegfried.

Darken upwards,
dusk of the gods !
Night of annulment,
near in thy cloud ! —
I stand in sight
of Siegfried's star ;
for me he was
and for me he will be,
own and always,
one and all ;
lighting love
and laughing death !

SIEGFRIED

(with BRÜNNHILDE).

Laughter awakes
the woman to me ;
Brünnhilde lives !
Brünnhilde laughs ! —

Hail the sun,
that sees us here !
Hail the day
we behold in heaven !
Hail the blaze,
that of night is born !
Hail the world,
where Brünnhild' awakes !
She wakes !   She lives !
She lures me with laughter !
Broadly strikes me
Brünnhilde's star !
For me she was
and for me she will be,
own and always,
one and all ;
lighting love
and laughing death !

BRÜNNHILDE throws herself into SIEGFRIED's arms.
The Curtain falls.

III. DIE MEISTERSINGER. — Act III.

(*a*) PRELUDE.
(*b*) HANS SACHS'S MONOLOGUE.
(*c*) QUINTET.
(*d*) CHORUS OF COBBLERS, TAILORS, AND BAKERS.
(*e*) DANCE OF APPRENTICES.
(*f*) PROCESSION OF MASTERSINGERS.
(*g*) CHORUS, " AWAKE ! "
(*h*) PRIZE SONG AND FINALE

THE hero of " Die Meistersinger " is a young knight, *Walter von Stolzing,* who beholds *Eva,* the lovely daughter of the goldsmith *Pogner,* in church. As usual in Wagner's operas, it is a case of mutual love at first sight. *Eva,* however, has been promised to the master who at a coming public singing-match shall win the prize. *Walter* accordingly resolves to join the guild of the Mastersingers ; but at his vocal examination his jealous rival, the old and conceited *Beckmesser,* notes down so many violations of the conventional and pedantic rules of the guild, that *Walter* is " black-balled." He then attempts an elopement, which is frustrated through the wise forethought of *Hans Sachs,* the famous cobbler-poet, the only one who had recognized the beauty of *Walter's* song, and who takes the Knight under his protection. *Walter* has a dream in *Sachs's* house, which he describes in the morning. It is the famous " prize-song," of which *Sachs* notes the words and music. *Beckmesser* gets hold of the copy by chance, thinks it is a new song by the popular *Sachs,* and endeavors to memorize it. But at the public singing-match, before the assembled people, he gets terribly " mixed up," and his voice is finally drowned in the derisive laughter of the audience. Then *Walter* comes forward, sings his dream-song, and is awarded the prize by public acclamation. The biographic significance of this plot lies on the surface. *Walter* with his new melody represents the " music of the future ; " the jealous *Beckmesser* the critics who condemn this music because it does not follow conventional rules of form ; and *Sachs* and the populace the more liberal opinion which recognizes the principle of progress and development in musical form.

The prelude to Act III. is one of the most exquisite of Wagner's tone-poems. It leads almost directly to the following famous monologue of *Sachs,* who sits in his room with a large book on his knees absorbed in deep thought.

SACHS'S MONOLOGUE.

Mad ! Mad !
All the world 's mad !
Where'er inquiry dives
In town or world's archives,
And seeks to learn the reason
Why people strive and fight,
Both in and out of season,
In fruitless rage and spite.
What do they gain
For all their pain ?
Repulsed in fight,
They feign joy in flight ;
Their pain-cries not minding,
They joy pretend

Die Meistersinger.

When their own flesh their fingers rend,
And pleasure deem they 're finding.
What tongue the cause can phrase?
'T is just the same old craze!
Nought haps without it ever,
In spite of all endeavor;
　　Pause doth it make,
In sleep it but acquires new force;
　　Soon it will wake,
Then lo! who can control its course? —
Old ways and customs keeping,
How peacefully I see
My dear old Nürnberg sleeping
In midst of Germany!
But on one evening late,
To hinder in some fashion
The follies of youthful passion,
A man worries his pate;
A shoemaker, all unknowing,
Sets the old madness going:
How soon from highways and alleys
A raging rabble sallies!
Man, woman, youth, and child,
Blindly fall to, as if gone wild;
　　And ere the craze lose power
　　The cudgel blows must shower;
　　They seek with fuss and pother
　　The fires of wrath to smother. —
　　God knows how this befell! —
　　'T was like some impish spell!
Some glow-worm could not find his mate;
'T was he aroused this wrath and hate. —
The elder's charm: — Midsummer-eve: —
But now has dawned Midsummer-day. —
Let 's see then what Hans Sachs can weave
To turn the madness his own way,
　　To serve for noble works;
　　For if still here it lurks,
　　In Nüremberg the same,
We 'll use it to such aim
As seldom by the mob 's projected,
And never without trick effected.

QUINTET.

Sachs calls his apprentice, David, and Eva's nurse, Magdalena, to witness the christening of Walter's dream-
song.

Sachs.

[That the melody lack not anything vital,
I now proceed to give it its title.]
" *The glorious morning-dream's true story.*" —
So be it named, to the Masters' glory.
And may it increase in size and strength. —
I bid the young god-mother speak at length.

Eva.

Dazzling as the dawn
That smiles upon my glee,
Rapture-laden morn
To bliss awakens me.
Dream of balmy beauty,
Brilliant morning-glow!
Hard but sweet 's the duty
Thy intent to know.
That divine and tender strain,
　With its tones of gladness,
Has revealed my heart's sweet pain,
　And subdued its sadness.
Is it but a morning-dream?
Scarcely real doth it seem.
　What the ditty,
　Soft and pretty,
　Told to me,
　A quiet theme,
　Loud and free,
In the Masters' conclave wise
Shall achieve the highest prize.

Walter.

'T was thy love — the highest gain —
Allured me by its gladness,
To reveal my heart's sweet pain
And subdue its sadness.
Is it still my morning-dream?
Scarcely real doth it seem.
　What the ditty,
　Soft and pretty,
　Told to thee,
　A quiet theme,
　Loud and free,
In the Masters' conclave wise
Shall achieve the highest prize.

Sachs.

With the maiden I would fain
Sing for very gladness;
But my heart I must restrain,
Quell my passion's madness.
'T was a tender evening-dream:
Undiscovered let it beam.
　What the ditty,
　Soft and pretty,
　Told to me
　In quiet theme,
　Here I see:
Youth and love that never dies
Flourish through the Master-prize.

David.

Am I awake, or dreaming still?
Scarce to explain it have I skill.
Sure 't is but a morning-dream!
All these things unreal seem.

Can it be, man,
You're a freeman?
And that she —
Oh, joy supreme! —
My spouse shall be?
Round and round my head-piece flies,
That a Master I now rise!

MAGDALENA.

Am I awake, or dreaming still?
Scarce to explain it have I skill.
Sure 't is but a morning-dream!
All these things unreal seem.
Can it be, man,
You're a freeman?
And that we —
Oh, joy supreme! —
Shall wedded be?
Yes; what honor near me lies!
Soon I shall as Madam rise!

*The orchestra goes into a broad, march-like theme.
SACHS makes the group break up.*

SACHS.

Now let's be off! — Your father stays!
Quick, to the fields all go your ways!

*(EVA tears herself away from SACHS and WALTER, and
leaves the house with MAGDALENA.)*

So come, Sir Knight! take heart of grace! —
David, my man, lock up the place!

*As SACHS and WALTER also go into the street, and
DAVID is left shutting up the shop, curtains descend from
each side of the proscenium so as to conceal the stage.
When the music has gradually swelled to the loudest
pitch, the curtains are drawn up again, and the scene is
changed.*

CHANGE OF SCENE.

*The stage now represents an open meadow; in the dis-
tance, at back, the town of Nuremberg. The Pegnitz
winds across the plain; the narrow river is "practicable" in
the foreground. Boats, gayly decorated with flags, continually discharge fresh parties of BURGHERS of the different
Guilds, with their wives and families, who land on the
banks. A raised stand, with benches on it, is erected R.,
already adorned with flags of those as yet arrived; as the
scene opens, the Standard-bearers of freshly-arriving Guilds
also place their banners against the Singers' stage, so that
it is at last quite closed in on three sides by them. Tents
with all kinds of refreshments border the sides of the open
space in front.*

*Before the tents is much merry-making; BURGHERS and
their families sit and group round them. The PRENTICES
of the MASTERSINGERS, in holiday attire, finely decked out
with ribbons and flowers, and bearing slender wands, also
ornamented, fulfil frolicsomely the office of heralds and
stewards. They receive the new-comers on the bank,
arrange them in procession, and conduct them to the
stand, whence, after the Standard-bearer has deposited his
banner, the BURGHERS and JOURNEYMEN disperse under
the tents.*

*Among the arriving Guilds the following are promi-
nent: —*

THE SHOEMAKERS

(as they march past).

Saint Crispin!
Honor him!
He was both wise and good,
Did all a cobbler could.
That was a fine time for the poor!
He made them all warm shoes;
When none would lend him leather more,
To steal he 'd not refuse.
The cobbler has a conscience easy,
No obstacles to labor sees he;
When from the tanner 't is sent away,
Then hey! hey! hey!
Leather becomes his rightful prey.

*The TOWN-PIPERS,. LUTE and TOY-INSTRUMENT-
MAKERS, playing on their instruments, follow. These
are succeeded by*

THE TAILORS.

When Nuremberg besieged did stand,
And famine wrought despair,
Undone had been both folk and land,
Had not a tailor been there,
Of craft and courage rare.
Within a goat-skin he did hide,
And showed upon the wall outside;
There took to gayly tripping
And gambolling and skipping.
The foe beheld it with dismay:
"The devil fetch that town away,
Where goats yet merrily play, play, play."
Me-ey! me-ey! me-ey!

(Imitating the bleating of a goat.)

Who'd think that a tailor within there lay?

THE BAKERS

*(coming close behind the TAILORS, so that the two songs
join together).*

Want of bread! Want of bread!
That is a hardship true, sirs!
If you were not by the baker fed,
Old Death would feed on you, sirs.
Pray! pray! pray!
Baker, ev'ry day,
Hunger take away!

PRENTICES.

Heyday! heyday! Maidens from Fürth!
Play up, Town-piper! One merry spurt!

*A gayly painted boat, filled with young GIRLS in fine
peasant costumes, arrives. The PRENTICES help the
GIRLS out, and dance with them, while the TOWN-PIPERS
play, towards the front. The character of this dance
consists in the PRENTICES appearing only to wish to bring
the GIRLS to the open place; the JOURNEYMEN endeavor*

to capture them, and the PRENTICES move on as if seeking another place, thus making the tour of the stage, and continually delaying their original purpose in fun and frolic.

DAVID
(advancing from the landing-place).

You dance ?   The Masters will rate such folly.

(The boys make faces at him.)

Don't care ?— Why then let me too be jolly !

He seizes a young and pretty girl, and mingles in the dance with great ardor. The spectators notice him, and laugh.

SOME OF THE PRENTICES.
David, here's Lena! There's Lena sees you !

DAVID
(alarmed, hastily releases the maiden ; but seeing nothing, quickly regains his courage and resumes his dancing).

Have done with your silly jokes, my boys, do !

JOURNEYMEN
(at the landing-place).

The Mastersingers ! The Mastersingers !

DAVID.
O ! lor'!— Farewell, ye pretty clingers !

He gives the maiden an ardent kiss, and tears himself away. The PRENTICES quickly discontinue their dance, hasten to the bank, and arrange themselves to receive the MASTERSINGERS. All stand back, by command of the PRENTICES. The MASTERSINGERS arrange their procession on the bank, and then march forwards to take their places on the stand. First, KOTHNER, as Standard-bearer ; then POGNER, leading EVA by the hand. She is attended by richly dressed MAIDENS, among whom is MAGDALENA. Then follow the other MASTERSINGERS. They are greeted with cheers and waving of hats. When all have reached the platform, EVA has taken the place of honor, with her MAIDENS round her, and KOTHNER has placed his banner in the middle of the others, which it over-tops, the PRENTICES solemnly advance, in rank and file, before the stand, turning to the people.

PRENTICES.
Silentium ! Silentium !
Make no sound, e'en the merest hum !

SACHS rises and steps forward. At sight of him all burst out into fresh acclamations and wavings of hats and kerchiefs.

ALL THE PEOPLE.
Ha ! Sachs ! 'T is Sachs !
See ! Master Sachs !
Sing all ! Sing all ! Sing all !
(With solemn delivery.)
" Awake ! Draws nigh the break of day :
I hear upon the hawthorn spray
A bonny little nightingale ;
His voice resounds o'er hill and dale.
The night descends the western sky,
And from the east the morn draws nigh ;
With ardor red the flush of day
Breaks through the cloud-bank dull and gray."
Hail Sachs ! Hans Sachs !
Hail, Nuremberg's darling Sachs !

The scene of *Beckmesser's* fiasco is omitted, as being too much dependent on comic action to be effective in the concert hall. *Beckmesser* attempts to excuse his failure by charging Sachs with the authorship of his song.

SACHS.
I am accused, and must defend :
A witness let me bid attend ! —
Is there one here who knows I 'm right,
Let him appear before our sight !

(WALTER advances from out the crowd.)
(General stir.)

Bear witness, the song is not by me ;
And prove to all that, in the plea
   I have advanced for it,
   I said but what was fit.

THE MASTERS.
Ah, Sachs ! You 're very sly indeed !
But you may for this once proceed.

SACHS.
It shows our rules are of excellence rare,
If now and then exceptions they'll bear.

PEOPLE.
A noble witness, proud and bold !
Methinks he should some good unfold.

SACHS.
Masters and people all agree
To give my witness liberty.
Sir Walter von Stolzing, sing the song !
You, Masters, see if he goes wrong.

He gives the MASTERS the paper to follow with.

PRENTICES.
All are intent, hushed is the hum ;
So we need not call out Silentium !

WALTER
(who has mounted the mound with proud and firm steps).
" Morning was gleaming with roseate light,
   The air was filled
   With scent distilled,

Die Meistersinger.

Where, beauty-beaming,
Past all dreaming,
A garden did invite,"—

(The MASTERS, here absorbed, let fall the leaf; WALTER
notices it without seeming to do so, and now proceeds in
a freer style)

" Wherein, beneath a wondrous tree,
With fruit superbly laden,
In blissful love-dream I could see
The rare and tender maiden,
Whose charms, beyond all price,
Entranced my heart —
Eva, in Paradise."

THE PEOPLE
(softly to one another).

That is quite diff'rent! Who would surmise
That so much in performance lies?

THE MASTERSINGERS
(softly aside).

Ah yes! I see! 't is another thing
A song the proper way to sing.

SACHS.

Witness in place!
Sing apace!

WALTER.

" Evening was darkling, and night closed around;
By rugged way
My feet did stray
Towards a mountain,
Where a fountain
Enslaved me with its sound;
And there, beneath a laurel-tree,
With starlight glinting under,
In waking vision greeted me —
A sweet and solemn wonder;
She dropped on me the fountain's dews,
That woman fair —
Parnassus' glorious Muse."

THE PEOPLE
(still more softly, aside).

How sweet it is! how true to Art!
And yet it touches every heart.

MASTERS.

'T is bold and daring, that is true;
But well composed, and vocal too.

SACHS.

A third time, witness, I commend;
Sing along, and end!

WALTER
(with great exaltation).

" Thrice happy day,
To which my poet's trance gave place!

That Paradise of which I dreamed,
In radiance new before my face
Glorified lay.
To point the path the brooklet streamed:
She stood beside me,
Who shall my bride be,
The fairest sight earth e'er gave,
My Muse, to whom I bow,
So angel-sweet and grave.
I woo her boldly now,
Before the world remaining,
By might of music gaining
Parnassus and Paradise!"

PEOPLE
(accompanying the close, very softly).

I feel as in a lovely dream,
Hearing, but grasping not the theme!
Give him the prize!
Maiden, rise!
No one could woo in nobler wise!

MASTERS.

Yes, glorious singer! Victor rise!
Your song has won the Master-prize!

POGNER.

O Sachs! All this I owe to you:
My happiness revives anew.

EVA, who from the commencement of the scene has
preserved a calm composure, and has seemed rapt from
all that passed around, has listened to WALTER immovably;
but now, when at the conclusion both MASTERS and PEOPLE
express their involuntary admiration, she rises, advances to
the edge of the platform, and places on the brow of WAL-
TER, who kneels on the steps, a wreath of myrtle and laurel;
whereupon he rises, and she leads him to her father, before
whom they both kneel. POGNER extends his hands in
benediction over them.

SACHS
(pointing to the group).

My witness answered not amiss!
Do you find fault with me for this?

PEOPLE
(jubilantly).

Hans Sachs! No! It was well devised!
Your tact you 've once more exercised!

SEVERAL MASTERSINGERS.

Now, Master Pogner! As you should,
Give him the honor of Masterhood!

POGNER
(bringing forward a gold chain with three medallions).

Receive King David's likeness true:
The Masters' Guild is free to you.

WALTER

(shrinking back involuntarily).

A Master! Nay!
I'll find reward some other way!

The MASTERS look disconcertedly towards SACHS.

SACHS

(grasping WALTER by the hand).

Disparage not the Masters' ways,
But show respect to Art!
All they can give of highest praise
To you they would impart.
Not through your ancestors and birth,
Not by your weapon's strength and worth,
But by a poet's brain
Which Mastership did gain,
You have attained your present bliss;
Then think you thankfully on this, —
How can you e'er the Art despise
Which can bestow so rare a prize? —
That by our Masters she was kept
And cherished as their own,
With anxious care that never slept.
This Art herself has shown,
If not so honored as of yore,
When courts and princes prized her more,
In troublous years all through
She's German been and true;
And if she has not won renown
Beyond this bustling busy town,

You see she has our full respect:
What more from us can you expect?
Beware! Bad times are nigh at hand:
And when fall German folk and land
In spurious foreign pomp ere long,
No prince will know his people's tongue;
And foreign thoughts and foreign ways
Upon our German soil they'll raise.
Our native Art will fade from hence
If 't is not held in reverence.
So heed my words!
Honor your German Masters
If you would stay disasters!
For while they dwell in every heart,
Though should depart
The pride of holy Rome,
Still thrives at home
Our sacred German Art!

All join enthusiastically in the last verse. EVA takes the crown from WALTER's head and places it on SACHS's; he takes the chain from POGNER's hand and puts it round WALTER's neck. WALTER and EVA lean against SACHS, one on each side; POGNER sinks on his knee before him as if in homage. The MASTERSINGERS point to SACHS with outstretched hands, as to their chief. While the PRENTICES clap hands and shout and dance, the people wave hats and kerchiefs in enthusiasm.

ALL.

Hail, Sachs! Hans Sachs.
Hail Nuremberg's darling Sachs!

The Curtain falls.

I. THE FLYING DUTCHMAN.

(a) Overture. — Act I.
(b) Introduction, Spinning Chorus and Ballad. — Act II.

THE overture to "The Flying Dutchman," like Beethoven's third Leonora overture, and like the prelude to "Lohengrin" and the overture to "Tannhäuser," is a complete symphonic poem or miniature drama, embodying the principal events of the play following it. Never before had a composer succeeded in making such a terribly vivid translation into artistic tones of raging ocean storms ; and "since Byron," says Liszt, "no poet has conceived such a pale phantom in gloomy night as Wagner with his *Dutchman*." The storm-music of "The Flying Dutchman" has been copied by most modern composers because it is so true to nature, being the outcome of impressions made on Wagner early in his career. In 1839 he embarked from North Prussia for London. The journey lasted three weeks and a half, and three terrible storms were encountered. On this trip Wagner read Heine's legend of "The Flying Dutchman," — the unhappy mariner, who, after trying long in vain to pass the Cape of Good Hope, had sworn that he would not desist if he had to sail on the ocean to eternity. To punish his blasphemy he was condemned to the fate of the Wandering Jew, his only hope of salvation lying in his release through the devotion unto death of a woman ; and to find such a maiden he is allowed every seven years to go on shore. On the occasion of his last visit he encounters the Norwegian captain, *Daland*, on whom his treasures make a great impression, and who promises him the hand of his daughter *Senta*. Through a picture of the *Dutchman* which hangs in her room *Senta* has become familiar with his features and his fate, and is attracted to him by an irresistible feeling of sympathy and love. She agrees to become his ; but in a farewell interview with *Erik*, a former admirer of hers, she is overheard by the *Dutchman*, who misinterprets her words, thinks he is betrayed again, and in terrible despair boards his phantom ship and sails away. But *Senta*, escaping from her friends, throws herself into the ocean ; and by her death releases from his curse the *Dutchman*, whose vessel immediately falls into pieces and vanishes, while the two lovers are seen rising heavenward, transfigured.

67

SPINNING CHORUS.

A large room in DALAND'S house; on the wall, pictures of sea-subjects, charts, etc.; on the farther wall the portrait of a pale man with a dark beard, in a black Spanish dress. MARY and the MAIDENS are sitting round the chamber and spinning. SENTA, leaning back in an armchair, is absorbed in dreamy contemplation of the portrait on the farther wall.

CHORUS OF MAIDENS.

Hum, hum, hum! good wheel, be whirling!
Gayly, gayly turn thee round!
Spin, spin, spin! the threads be twirling!
Turn, good wheel, with humming sound!
My love now sails on distant seas;
His faithful heart for home doth yearn;
Couldst thou, good wheel, but give the breeze,
My love would soon to me return!
Spin, spin, spin! spin we duly!
Hum, hum! wheel, go truly!
Tra la ra la la la la la!

MARY.

Ah, duly, duly are they spinning!
Each girl a sweetheart would be winning!

THE MAIDENS.

Dame Mary, hush! for well you know
Our song as yet must onward go!
You know as yet our song must onward go!

MARY.

Then sing, yet ply a busy wheel.
But wherefore, Senta, art thou still?

THE MAIDENS.

Hum, hum, hum! good wheel be whirling, etc.
On distant seas my love doth sail;
In southern lands much gold he wins!
Then turn, good wheel, nor tire, nor fail;
The gold for her who duly spins!
Spin we duly! wheel go truly!
Tra la ra la la la la la!

MARY
(to SENTA).

Thou careless girl! Wilt thou not spin?
Thy lover's gift thou wilt not win.

MAIDENS.

She has no need to work as we;
Her lover sails not on the sea;
He brings her game instead of gold!
One knows the worth of hunters bold!
(laughing).
Ha ha ha ha ha ha ha!

SENTA sings softly to herself.

MARY.

You see her! Still before that face!
Why wilt thou dream away thy girlhood
With gazing at that picture so?

SENTA
(without changing her position).

Why hast thou told me of his sorrows?
His hapless fate why did I know?
(sighing).
The wretched man!

MARY.

God help thee, girl!

MAIDENS.

Ei, ei! Ei, ei! What's that she said?
Her sighs are for the ghastly man!
'T is brooding makes her look so wan!

MARY.

I fear that she will lose her head!
No use for me to chide each day!
Come! Senta, wilt thou turn away?

MAIDENS.

She hears you not! She is in love!
She is in love! in love!
Ei ei! Ei ei! No anger pray it move!
For Erik has a temper hot;
And if his heart will bear it not!
Say nought! Lest in a rage he fall,
And shoot his rival on the wall!

They laugh.

SENTA
(starting up angrily).

Be still with all your foolish jesting!
My temper are you bent on testing?

The MAIDENS sing as loud as possible, and turn their spinning-wheels with great noise, so as to give SENTA no opportunity of complaining.

THE MAIDENS.

Hum, hum, hum! good wheel be whirling!
Gayly, gayly turn thee round!
Spin, spin, spin! the threads be twirling!
Turn, good wheel, with humming sound!

SENTA.

Oh! make an end of all this singing!
Your hum, hum, hum! quite tires my ear!
If me you would your way be bringing,
Provide some better thing to hear!

MAIDENS.

Well, sing thyself!

SENTA.

Much would I rather Dame Mary sang to us the ballad.

MARY.

I'd rather not attempt the thing!
The Flying Dutchman let him be!

SENTA.

The song I oft have heard you sing
I'll sing myself!

I 'd rather not attempt the thing !
Hark, then, to me !
A tale of sorrow I select you :
His wretched fate, it must affect you !

MAIDENS.

Well, let us hear.
And we will rest !

MARY

(peevishly).

I 'll spin away !

The MAIDENS move their seats nearer to the armchair, after they have put aside their spinning-wheels, and group themselves round SENTA. MARY remains sitting where she was, and goes on spinning.

BALLAD.

SENTA

(in the armchair).

Yo-ho-ho ! Yo-ho-ho-ho !
Yo-ho-ho ! Yo-ho !
A ship the restless ocean sweeps ;
Blood-red her sails, and black her masts ;
Her spectral captain never sleeps,
But watchful glance round him casts.
Hui ! The wind is shrill !
Yo-ho-he ! Yo-ho-he ! Hui !
The wind is shrill ! Yo-ho-he ! Yo-ho-he ! Hui !
Like an arrow he flies, without aim, without rest,
without end.
Yet this the spectral man from his life-long curse
may deliver,
Find he a maiden, faithful and true, to love him
forever.
Ah, mightest thou, spectral seaman, but find
her !
Pray ye that Heaven may soon at his need grant
him this boon.

(Towards the end of the verse SENTA turns to the picture. The MAIDENS listen with interest. MARY has left off spinning.)

Against a temper's utmost wrath,
Around a Cape he once would sail.
He cursed and swore a foolish oath :
Befall what may, I will prevail !
Hui ! And Satan heard ! Yo-ho-he !
Yo-ho-he ! Hui !
He mark'd his word.
Yo-ho-he ! Yo-ho-he ! Hui !
And condemned him to sail on the sea without
aim, without end.
Yet this the wretched man from his life-long curse
may deliver,
Would but an angel show him the way his bond-
age to sever.

MAIDENS

(with emotion).

Ah ! mightest thou, spectral seaman, but find it !
Pray ye that Heaven may soon at his need grant
him this boon !

SENTA

(who, at the second verse had risen from the chair, comes
forward with increasing agitation).

He lands at every seventh year's end,
A wife to seek he wanders round ;
But wheresoe'er his steps he bend,
For him no faithful wife is found.
Hui ! Unfurl the sails ! Yo-ho-he ! Yo-ho-he !
Hui ! The anchor weigh ! Yo-ho-he !
Yo-ho-he ! Hui ! Faithless love ! Faithless troth !
To the sea, without aim, without end !

SENTA, exhausted, sinks back in the chair. After a deep
pause the MAIDENS go on singing softly.

MAIDENS.

Ah ! where is she, to whose loving heart the
angel may guide thee ?
Where lingers she, thine own unto death, whatever betide thee ?

SENTA

(carried away by a sudden inspiration, and springing up
from the chair).

I am the one who through her love will save
thee !
Oh may the angel hither guide thee !
Through me may new-found joy betide thee !

MARY.

Heaven help us ! Senta !

MAIDENS

(springing up, terrified).

Heaven help us ! Senta ! Senta !

[ERIK

(who is entering at the door, and has heard SENTA's
outcry).

Senta ! Wouldst thou then forsake me ?]

MAIDENS.

Help, Erik, help ! This must be madness !

MARY.

This outburst fills my heart with sadness !
Abhorred picture, thou shalt burn,
Let but her father once return !

[ERIK

(sadly).

Her father comes.]

69

SENTA

(who has remained motionless and absorbed, springs up
joyfully as if awaking).

My father here?

[ERIK.

From off the height I saw his sail.]

MARY

(in a great bustle).

How idle shall we all appear,
If we in household duties fail !

(Detaining the MAIDENS.)

Hold! hold! With me you ought to stay.
The sailors come with urgent hunger;
For food and wine they soon will ask.
Restrain yourselves a little longer !
Nor leave undone each needful task !

THE MAIDENS.

We at work cannot stay much longer !
There is so much we want to ask !
Enough we satisfy their hunger,
Then we have done each needful task.

II. DIE MEISTERSINGER.

(*a*) VORSPIEL.
(*b*) POGNER'S ADDRESS. — ACT II.

A BRIEF sketch of " Die Meistersinger " will be found on page 61. *Pogner* is the
oldest of the Mastersingers, and in the following address to his colleagues
announces that he will give his daughter and all his wealth to the winner of the prize
at the coming vocal contest.

POGNER.

Then hear, and mark me well!
St. John's most holy festal day,
Ye know, we keep to-morrow ;
In meadows green, among the hay,
With song and dance and merry play,
Each heart will gladness borrow
And cast aside all sorrow ;
So each will sport as best he may.
The Singing-school we Masters here
A staid church-choir will christen :
From out the gates, with merry cheer,
To open meadows we will steer,
While festal banners glisten :
The populace shall listen
To Master-Songs with layman's ear.
For those who best succeed in song
Are gifts of various sizes,
And all will hail, full loud and long,
Both melodies and prizes.
I am, thank God ! a wealthy man ;
And, as each giveth what he can,
I've ransacked ev'ry coffer
To find a prize to offer,
To shame not to be brought.
Now hear what I've bethought.

Through German lands when I have roved
It pained me, as I listed,
To hear the burghers are not loved,
Deemed selfish and close-fisted.
In low life, as in courts the same,
I always heard the bitter blame
That only treasure and gold
The burgher's thoughts can hold.
That we in all Empire's bounds
Alone have Art promoted,
I fancy they scarcely have noted:
But how this to our honor redounds,
And how, with proudest care,
We treasure the good and rare,
What Art is worth, what it can do,
Now have I a mind to show unto you.
So hear, Masters, what thing
As a prize I mean to bring : —
The singer, to whose lyric skill
The public voice the prize shall will,
On John the Baptist's day, —
Be he whoe'er he may, —
I, Pogner, an Art-supporter,
A townsman of this quarter,
Will give, with my gold and goods beside,
Eva, my only child, for bride.

Götterdämmerung.

III. GÖTTERDÄMMERUNG.

(a) SIEGFRIED AND THE RHINE MAIDENS.
(b) STORY OF SIEGFRIED'S LIFE.
(c) MURDER SCENE AND DEAD MARCH.
(d) BRÜNNHILDE'S SELF IMMOLATION.

HE Dusk of the Gods, the last part of the tetralogy, consists of three acts and two short preludes. In one of these preludes we see once more *Brünnhilde* on the rock, where she had lain during her magnetic sleep, and where *Siegfried* had found her and taken her as his wife. *Siegfried* makes up his mind to leave her for a while in quest of adventures. He gives her the Nibelung's ring as a pledge of faith. He had obtained it when he slew the dragon *Fafner*, and, as the sequel will show, he was doomed to suffer the consequences of the fatal curse which was invoked on every possessor of the ring when *Wotan* took it away from the Nibelung dwarf *Alberich*, who had originally made it out of the gold of the Rhine.

Siegfried joyously sets out on his journey, and soon comes to the Court of *King Gunther* on the Rhine. *Gunther's* half-brother, *Hagen*, is the son of *Alberich*, and anxious to restore the ring to his father. Through his artful devices *Siegfried* is made to drink a love-potion, which causes him to forget *Brünnhilde* and marry the *King's* sister, *Gutrune*. In return for his sister's hand, *Gunther* asks *Siegfried* to bring *Brünnhilde* to him as wife. The possession of the tarnhelmet enables *Siegfried* to assume the form of *Gunther*, and in this form he overcomes *Brünnhilde* and brings her to *Gunther*. In the struggle he takes away her ring: by this it is that she subsequently knows that it was he who brought her to *Gunther*. She accordingly accuses him of perfidy, and it is resolved that *Siegfried* must die. A grand hunting expedition is organized. *Siegfried* gets separated from his companions [Act III.], and encounters the *Rhine Daughters*, who vainly beg him for his ring, after telling him of the curse that pursues every unrightful possessor of it. After rejoining his companions they all make halt for rest and refreshments. *Siegfried* sits and tells of his early youth and his adventures with *Mime*, the dragon *Fafner*, and the bird that guided him to the rock of the Walkyrie, — a charming musical and poetic synopsis of the whole "Siegfried" drama. His memory revives, and he tells of his wooing of *Brünnhilde*, to the consternation of *Gunther*, when *Hagen* suddenly rises and stabs *Siegfried* in the back as he turns around to look after two ravens that suddenly fly over him. These and the remaining scenes, — the carrying of his body up the hill in the moonlight, the grief of *Gutrune*, and the self-immolation of *Brünnhilde*, will be found in the text of the third act, which is here printed entire, although the vocal part within brackets will be omitted at the concert.

SIEGFRIED WARNED BY THE RHINE DAUGHTERS.

(GÜTTERDÄMMERUNG.)

Götterdämmerung.

BRÜNNHILDE

(alone in the middle; after she has for a long while, at first with a deep shudder, then with almost overpowering sadness, contemplated SIEGFRIED'S face, she turns with solemn exaltation to the men and women).

Build me with logs
aloft on his brim
a heap for the Rhine to heed;
fast and far
tower the flame,
as it licks the limbs
the highest hero has left! —
His horse guide to my hand,
to be gone with me to his master;
for amidst his holiest   .
meed to be with him
I long in every limb. —
Fulfil Brünnhilde's bent!

The younger men, during what follows, raise a great funeral pile in front of the hall, near the bank of the Rhine; women dress it with hangings, on which they strew herbs and flowers.

BRÜNNHILDE

(again lost in contemplation of SIEGFRIED's body).

Like a look of sun
he sends me his light;
his soul was faultless
that false I found!
His bride he betrayed
by truth to his brother,
and from her whose haunt
was wholly his bosom,
barred himself with his sword. —
Sounder than his,
are oaths not sworn with;
better than his,
held never are bargains;
holier than his,
love is unheard of;
and yet to all oaths,
to every bargain,
to faithfullest love too —
has lied never his like! —

See you how it was so? —

O you, who heed
our oaths in your heaven,
open your eyes
on the bloom of my ill —
and watch your unwithering blame!
For my summons hark,
thou highest God!
Him, by his daringest deed —
that filled so fitly thy hope,
darkly thy means
doomed in its midst
to ruin's merciless wrong;
me, too,

to betray he was bounden,
that a wise woman might be!
Guess I not now of thy good? —

Nothing! Nothing!
Nought is hidden;
all is owned to me here!
Fitly thy ravens
take to their feathers;
with tidings dreadly dreamed for,
hence to their home they shall go.
Slumber! slumber, thou god!

She signs to the men to lift SIEGFRIED's body and bear it to the funeral pile: at the same time she draws the ring from SIEGFRIED's finger, contemplates it during what follows, and at last puts it on her own.

My heirdom here
behold me hallow!

Thou guilty ring!
Ruining gold!
My hand gathers,
and gives thee again.
You wisely seeing
water-sisters,
the Rhine's unresting Daughters,
I deem your word was of weight!
All that you ask
now is your own;
here from my ashes'
heap you may have it!
The flame as it clasps me round,
free from its curse the ring!
Back to its gold
unbind it again,
and far in the flood
withhold its fire,
the Rhine's unslumbering sun,
that for harm from him was reft.

(She turns towards the back. where SIEGFRIED's body lies already on the pile, and seizes from a man the great firebrand.)

Away, you ravens!
Whisper to your master
what here among us you heard!
By Brünnhilde's rock
your road shall be bent;
who roars yet round it,
Loge, warn him to Walhall!
For with doom of gods
is darkened the day;
so — set I the torch
To Walhall's towering walls.

(She flings the brand into the heap of wood, which quickly blazes up. Two ravens have flown up from the bank, and disappear towards the background. Two young men bring in the horse; BRÜNNHILDE seizes and quickly unbridles it.)

Grane, my horse,
hail to thee here!

Götterdämmerung.

Knowest thou, friend,
how far I shall need thee ?
Behold how lightens
hither thy lord,
Siegfried, my sorrowless hero.
To go to him now
neigh'st thou so gladly ?
Lure thee to him
the light and the laughter ?
Feel how my bosom
fills with its blaze !
Hands of fire
hold me at heart ;
fully to fold him,
to feel I am felt,
in masterless love
to be laid to his limbs !
Heiaho ! Grane !
Greeting to him !
Siegfried ! Brünnhilde see !
Happy hails thee thy bride !

She has swung herself stormily on to the horse, and rides it with a leap into the burning pile. The flame at once soars crackling on high, so that the fire fills the whole space in front of the hall, and seems almost to seize on the hall itself. In terror the women press to the foreground. Suddenly the fire sinks, so that nothing but a gloomy heat-cloud remains hanging over the place ; this rises and completely parts. The Rhine has violently swollen forward from its bank, and rolls its water over the place of the fire, up to the threshold of the hall. The THREE RHINE DAUGHTERS have swum forward on its waves. HAGEN, who since what happened with the ring has in growing anxiety watched BRÜNNHILDE's demeanor, at the sight of the RHINE DAUGHTERS is seized with the greatest dread ; he hurriedly flings away spear, shield, and helmet, and with the cry, " Unhand the Ring ! " plunges, as if out of his senses, into the flood. WOGLINDE and WELLGUNDE wind his neck in their arms, and so draw him with them as they swim back into the deep ; FLOSSHILDE, in front of the others, holds exultingly on high the ring which she has seized. — In the sky, at the same time, breaks out from the distance a reddish glow like the Northern Light, which grows continually broader and stronger. — The men and women, in speechless commotion, watch both the action and the appearance in the sky. — The Curtain falls.

I. HULDIGUNGSMARSCH.

THIS march, as its name implies, is an expression of Wagner's homage to the King of Bavaria. It was written in 1861, shortly after the King had invited him to Munich and made him a present of a villa at the Starnberger See, near the city.

II. LOHENGRIN.

ACT I.

(a) PRELUDE (*Orchestra*).

ACT II.

(b) ELSA AND ORTRUD. — GRAND DUO. — SCENE II.
(c) BRIDAL CHORUS: "MAY EVERY JOY ATTEND THEE." — SCENE IV.

ACT III.

(d) INTRODUCTION (*Orchestra*).
(e) CHORUS, "FAITHFUL AND TRUE." — SCENE I.
(f) GRAND DUO — LOHENGRIN AND ELSA. — SCENE II.
(g) MARCH (*Orchestra and Chorus*). — SCENE III.

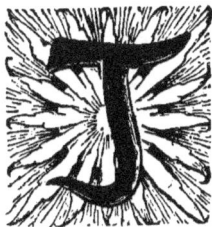

THE two operas included in Wednesday's programme are related in so far as they may both be regarded as predecessors of "Lohengrin." More closely related still are the two operas on to-day's programme. *Parsifal* is the father of *Lohengrin;* and although more than thirty years intervened between the composition of these two works, and their dramatic style is widely different, there are nevertheless numerous points of resemblance, such as the ethereal Grail harmonies, the swan motive, and a general sweet and placid character which belongs to both dramas. Wherever opera is sung the story is known of the knight *Lohengrin*, who comes on his swan-boat to defend *Elsa* from the accusation by Count *Telramund* and *Ortrud*, of having murdered her young brother, in order to become ruler of the land in his stead. *Lohengrin* vanquishes *Telramund* in combat, and thus establishes the innocence of *Elsa*, who becomes his wife. But *Ortrud* succeeds in implanting in her breast a suspicion and curiosity as to her husband's origin; and although *Elsa* has promised never to ask whence he came, on penalty of losing him, she questions him in the bridal chamber; whereupon the knight, in accordance with his vow, leaves her and departs on his swan-boat.

The great duo (*f*) is always shortened at the performances of Italian opera in this country, and will be heard here for the first time entire. The duo (*b*) is in Wagner's latest dramatic vein, — full of passionate realism, rich orchestral color, and exuberant melody. The famous prelude symbolizes the descent from heaven of a group of angels bearing the Holy Grail. Coming nearer and nearer, they fill the air with the blessings of the holy cup as with intoxicating perfumes. The senses are overwhelmed, and all sink down in ecstatic worship as the sounds grow louder and louder. Having dispensed their blessings, the angels again move heavenward; and as they pass out of sight the sounds die away *pianissimo*, as they had commenced. This, in a few words, is Wagner's own explanation. Attention may be called to the fact that no city has ever had the privilege of hearing on the same evening three singers so famous in the *rôles* of *Elsa*, *Ortrud*, and *Lohengrin*, as Nilsson, Materna, and Winkelmann.

ACT II. — SCENE II.

ELSA

(in white garments, appears on the balcony; she steps forward to the parapet, and leans her head on her hand; FREDERICK and ORTRUD, opposite to her, sit on the steps of the Minster).

Ye wand'ring breezes heard me
When grief was all I knew;
Now, that delight hath stirr'd me,
My joy I'll breathe to you.
Thro' heav'n's azure ye bore him,
Ye wafted him to me;
'Mid stormy waves watch'd o'er him,
My guide, my love, to be.
Where'er thy pinion rusheth
The mourner's tears are dried;
My cheek, that burns and flusheth
With love, oh cool and hide!

ORTRUD.

Be near, ye Pow'rs of Darkness!
May she for ever rue this hour!
Away! thou must a while from hence depart!

FREDERICK.

But why?

ORTRUD.

Leave her for me; her knight shall be for you.

FREDERICK retires to the background.

ORTRUD

(calls in a plaintive voice).

Elsa!

ELSA.

Who calls? How drearily and strangely
My name resoundeth thro' the night!

ORTRUD.

Elsa!
Hast thou forgotten e'en my voice?
Wilt thou disown me in my sorrow,
Who am by thee of all bereft?

ELSA.

Ortrud, 't is thou! What dost thou here, woman unblest?

ORTRUD.

Woman unblest! Yea, thou hast cause, unblest to call me!
I dwelt in solitude protected,
My home the deep and silent wood.
I harm'd thee not, I harm'd thee not!
Joyless, I mourn'd the evil fortune
That long hath rested on my race.
I harm'd thee not! I harm'd thee not!

ELSA.

And why, why speak to me of this?
Thy sorrow was not caus'd by me!

ORTRUD.

'T were strange indeed if thou didst envy
My lot, to be the wife of him
Whom scornfully thy heart disdain'd.

ELSA.

Ye guardian saints! why this to me?

ORTRUD.

The victim of a wild delusion,
He dared to cast a doubt on thee.
Since then he by remorse is riven;
The ban is spoken o'er his head.

ELSA.

Have mercy, Heav'n!

ORTRUD.

   Thou canst be happy!
Thy brief and guileless morn of promise
Prepar'd thee for a radiant noon.
Depart from my unholy presence;
From thee I may not crave a boon.
I will not haunt thy future bright,
Nor darken thy undimm'd delight!

ELSA
(with emotion).

So blest I am, O bounteous Heaven,
So great the boon I owe to thee,
Ne'er from my side be sorrow driven,
When in the dust it sues to me!
No, never! Ortrud, wait thou there!
E'er long, again I shall be near!

She hastens back into the Kemenate; ORTRUD darts from
her seat on the Minster-steps in wild exultation.

ORTRUD.

Ye Gods, forsaken, grant, grant me your ven-
 geance!
Declare your pow'r, be nigh in this dread hour!
Strike them with death who profane your altars!
And strengthen my soul to avenge your wrongs!
Odin, thou strong and mighty one!
Freya, O Queen, bend down to me!
Prosper my cause with deadly guile!
Immortals, on my vengeance smile!

ELSA
(still outside).

Ortrud! where art thou?

ELSA, with two Maids bearing lights, enters by the lower
door.

ORTRUD
(humbly prostrating herself before ELSA).

Here, before thee kneeling!

ELSA.
(starting back at the sight of ORTRUD).

O Heaven! How sorely art thou stricken,
Whom I in pride and splendor saw!
My heart's compassion it doth quicken;
Heav'n's dark decree I mark with awe!
Arise! Oh, do not thus entreat me!
Wert thou my foe, I pardon thee;

And if through me thy heart hath sorrow'd,
I humbly ask thou pardon me!

ORTRUD.

My grateful thanks for all thy goodness!

ELSA.

Of him whom I shall wed at morn
Grace I'll crave for thee and thy husband:
A boon to me he'll not refuse.

ORTRUD.

Oh, hold my heart in grateful bondage!

ELSA
(with rising animation).

By morning's dawn be thou prepar'd;
Attire thyself in royal raiment;
With me before the altar go!
(With joyous pride.)
Then I shall meet my hero guide,
In face of Heav'n to be his bride.

ORTRUD.

How can I e'er for this requite thee,
Since I henceforth am poor and lone?
Though as thy friend thou dost invite me,
I must myself thy vassal own!
(Drawing nearer to ELSA.)
One gift alone the Gods have lent me
(None silence to me hath ordain'd):
With that perchance I may prevent thee
From treason and thy life's attaint!

ELSA
(artlessly and kindly).

What say'st thou?

ORTRUD
(vehemently).

As thy friend I warn thee, lest thou in love too
 blindly trust;
Lest cruel fortune change and spurn thee;
For its decrees are oft unjust.

ELSA.

What fortune?

ORTRUD
(with great mystery).

May he never leave thee,
Who was by magic hither brought;
And may the glamour ne'er deceive thee
That in thy soul his words have wrought.

ELSA
(turns away, seized with secret dread; then turns again to
ORTRUD, full of compassion).

Oh that thy heart could know the treasure
Of love that knows not fear or doubt!

No child of earth that bliss can measure
Who doth not dwell in faith devout.
Rest thee with me! Oh let me teach thee
How trust doth hallow joy and love!
Turn to our faith, I do beseech thee, —
Our faith divine, for God is love!

ORTRUD

(aside).

Oh pride of heart, I yet will teach thee
That an illusion is this love!
The Gods of vengeance soon shall reach thee!
Their wrath, destroying, thou shalt prove!

ORTRUD, conducted by ELSA, after some pretended scruples, enters through the lower door; the Maids precede them with lights, and when all have entered, lock the door. Beginning of daybreak.

———+———

SCENE IV.

A long train of LADIES, magnificently attired, proceed slowly from the Kememate, passing before the Palace; then returning to the front, they ascend the steps of the Minster, where they remain standing. ELSA appears amid the train; the Nobles deferentially bare their heads.

CHORUS.

May ev'ry joy attend thee,
Who long in grief wert bound;
May Heav'n its blessing lend thee,
And angels guard thee round!
She comes, with blushes glowing,
On holy thoughts intent!
Thine be a bliss o'erflowing!
Hail, Elsa of Brabant!

———+———

ACT III. — SCENE I.

The bridal chamber; to the right an oriel casement, which is open. Music behind the stage, at first heard quite in the distance, and gradually approaching nearer. At the middle of the strain doors at the back of the stage are opened; the LADIES enter, leading in ELSA, the KING and Nobles leading in LOHENGRIN; Pages with lights go before them.

CHORUS.

Faithful and true, we lead ye forth
Where Love, triumphant, shall crown ye with
joy!
Star of renown, flow'r of the earth,
Blest be ye both far from all life's annoy!
Champion victorious, go thou before!
Maid bright and glorious, go thou before!
Mirth's noisy revel ye 've forsaken,
Tender delights for you now awaken;
Fragrant abode enshrine ye in bliss;
Splendor and state in joy ye dismiss!

EIGHT LADIES

(after they have gone round once).

As solemn vows unite ye
We hallow ye to joy!
This hour shall still requite ye,
When bliss hath known alloy!
Faithful and true, now rest you here.

Here both trains have passed entirely from the stage; the last Pages that close the procession shut the doors.

———+———

SCENE II.

LOHENGRIN.

The blissful strain is o'er; we are alone;
The first and only time since we have met.
Now ev'ry pent-up thought our hearts may own;
No rash intruder this sweet hour shall fret.
Elsa, my love! my own, my gentle wife!
If thou art blest as I, oh say, sweet life?

ELSA.

Words cannot tell the rapture sweet and tender
That floods my soul with joy divine!
When thou dost bend o'er me thy glance of
splendor,
When thou art near, the bliss of heav'n is mine!

LOHENGRIN.

Thy words, O fairest! well thy transports render!
If thou art blest, thy joy is doubly mine!
Bend thou on me those eyes so soft and tender,
Oh let me breathe with thee a joy divine!

ELSA.

I feel a joy sweet and tender,
A joy divine, breathe this joy divine.

LOHENGRIN.

With charmed links did Heav'n to thee unite
me!
Ere yet we met, thy heart had dreamt of me;
And if as champion I was called to right thee,
'T was love alone that led my way to thee.
I knew thee pure from ev'ry taint of wrong;
To thee my heart and homage true belong.

ELSA.

I saw thee first from azure heights descending.
T' was in a dream thy form I first beheld;
When o'er my waking eyes I saw thee bending,
I knew thee sent as angels were of eld.
My heart with joy would fain dissolve before thee;
I 'd trace thy steps as brook thro' flow'ry mead;
Like od'rous roses, sweetness I 'd waft o'er thee.
Dying for thy dear sake were blest indeed!
Say do I love thee? By what blissful token
Is shown that pow'r so dread and yet so blest?

Lohengrin.

Or, like thy name, — ah, may it not be spoken ? —
Must what I prize the most be ne'er express'd ?

LOHENGRIN
(caressingly).

Elsa !

ELSA.

How sweet my name, as from thy lips it glided !
Canst thou deny to me the sound of thine ?
In blissful hour thou 'lt to my heart confide it,
That of thy love shall be the seal and sign !

LOHENGRIN.

O my sweet wife ! Softly, when none are nigh,
Whisper the word ; none e'er shall hear but I.

LOHENGRIN tenderly holds ELSA in his arm, and points
through the open casement to the flowery close below.

LOHENGRIN.

Say, dost thou breathe the incense sweet of
flow'rs,
Bearing a tide of sweet mysterious joy?
And wouldst thou know from whence this rap-
ture show'rs ?
Ask not ; lest thou the wondrous charm destroy !
Such is the magic that to thee hath bound me,
When I first beheld thy beauty past compare ;
Knowing thee not, I worshipp'd and renown'd
thee ;
I felt thy glance, and knew thee true as fair.
And as the od'rous gales with rapture fire me,
Borne on the dark, unfathom'd gloom of night,
Thus thou to trust unmeasur'd didst inspire me
When thou wert crush'd by dark Suspicion's
blight.

ELSA conceals her emotion by clinging devotedly to LO-
HENGRIN.

ELSA.

Ah! could I show my deep devotion,
Do some good deed worthy of thee !
Nought have I but my fond emotion ;
Never can I thy equal be !
Were doubt and danger low'ring o'er thee,
As once they threaten'd me with woe,
And I could to thy right restore thee,
Then might my heart some comfort know !
Haply thy secret 's fraught with danger,
Therefore thy lips to all are clos'd.
'T shall ne'er be known to friend or stranger,
If thou in me thy trust repose.
Doubt me not ! Oh, let me share it !
Oh, let me know thy faith complete !
Not death itself from me shall tear it ;
And torture borne for thee were sweet !

LOHENGRIN.

My lov'd one !

ELSA
(more and more impetuously).

Oh, make me glad with thy reliance !
Humble me not, that bend so low ;
Ne'er shalt thou rue thy dear alliance ;
Him that I love, oh, let me know !

LOHENGRIN.

No more, O Elsa !

ELSA
(more and more pressingly).

Tell, oh, tell me !
Reveal thy name, ador'd to love !
Thy race and name, all that befell thee ;
My power of silence thou shalt prove !

LOHENGRIN.

Greatest of trusts, O Elsa, I have shown thee,
When I believed thee true from ev'ry stain ;
Wav'ring in faith, if thou shouldst ever own
thee,
Thy empire o'er my heart thou't ne'er regain.

(He again turns fondly towards ELSA.)

Oh, let my arms in love enfold thee !
Come rest thee here, my love, my life !
Let me in radiant joy behold thee ;
Far from our hearts be thought of strife !
Come to my heart ! Oh, let me press thee !
Let me inhale thy od'rous breath !
Angels might glory to possess thee !
Oh, turn to me in loving faith !
Thy love alone for all consoles me,
That I for thy dear sake have lost.
A high and glorious fate controls me, —
The fate true knight must prize the most !
As when the King desir'd to crown me,
My heart disdain'd the proffer'd boon,
No earthly glory can renown me !
I glory in thy spirit borrow ;
Thy love is all the world to me !
I came not here from night and sorrow ;
From blest delights I came to thee.

ELSA.

Help, Heav'n ! What dost thou tell me !
What must thy lips relate !
With glamour thou'ds't beguile me ;
I know my wretched fate !
The lot thou hast forsaken
Is still thy heart's desire ;
One day I shall awaken,
When thou of me shalt tire.
Oh ! how can I believe thee ?
I know that we must part !
Of joy thy words bereave me ;
Hopes fade within my heart.

79

Lohengrin.

LOHENGRIN.

No more, oh, I beseech thee !

ELSA.

On thee I yet may gaze !
Until despair shall reach me,
Oh ! must I count the days ?
In dread my soul shall languish,
Lest from my sight thou fly.
Thou'lt leave me in my anguish, —
Of sorrow I shall die !

LOHENGRIN.

Thou ne'er for me shalt sorrow,
While thou from doubt art free !

ELSA.

What magic can I borrow
To bind thy heart to me ?
A spell is cast around thee ;
By magic thou art here !
What ties soe'er have bound thee
Thou by a spell canst tear !

(She suddenly starts, violently agitated, and pauses, listening.)

Hark ! There are sounds ! Oh, bend thy ear, and listen !

LOHENGRIN.

Elsa !

ELSA.

Alas ! 'T is there, the swan, the swan,
As when I first beheld his pinions glisten !
For thee he comes ! Ah, must thou now be gone !

LOHENGRIN.

Elsa, oh, hush ! What fancies vain are these ?

ELSA.

No ; thou shalt not compel me
To trust by words of blame !
No ; not unless thou tell me thy country and thy name !
What fatal spell is thine ?
In vain wouldst thou assure me.
Declare thy race and name !
Where is thy home ?

LOHENGRIN.

Elsa, oh, I conjure thee ! Forbear ! Woe's me !

ELSA perceives FREDERICK and his four associates, who break in, with drawn swords, through a door at the back.

ELSA.

Save thyself ! Thy sword ! thy sword !

She hands him his sword, which was by the side of the couch, so that while she holds the sheath he quickly draws it out, and with one blow strikes FREDERICK, whose arm is uplifted against him, dead. The four Nobles let fall their swords, and kneel before LOHENGRIN.
ELSA, who has sunk on LOHENGRIN's breast, faints, and slowly sinks to the ground. Long silence. LOHENGRIN, deeply moved, remains standing.

LOHENGRIN.

Woe ! all our joy now is fled for aye !

ELSA

(opening her eyes faintly).

Eternal One, have mercy thou !

On a sign from LOHENGRIN, the four Nobles rise.

LOHENGRIN.

Bear hence the corpse into the King's judgment hall !

(The four Nobles take up FREDERICK's corpse, and depart with it through the door. LOHENGRIN pulls a bell ; two Ladies enter.)

Into the royal presence lead her,
Array'd as fits so fair a bride !
There all she asks I will concede her,
Nor from her knowledge aught will hide.

He departs sadly and solemnly. The Ladies lead out ELSA, who is speechless. The day has slowly begun to dawn ; the tapers are extinguished ; a large Curtain is let down so as to cut off the stage entirely from view.

SCENE III.

When the Curtain is drawn aside, the scene represents the bank of the Scheldt, as in Act I. A brilliant dawn gradually brightens into full daylight. Several Counts enter in succession, announced by trumpets, and accompanied by their Vassals. Finally the King arrives, with the Saxon *Arrièr. ban.*

CHORUS.

Hail, royal Henry !
Royal Henry, hail !

www.ingramcontent.com/pod-product-compliance
Lightning Source LLC
Chambersburg PA
CBHW022153090426
42742CB00010B/1496